The Glynn's —

All the BEST!

"We may have a hearing loss, but our hearing loss does not have us!"

J/11/

Hearing with my Heart

The JUSTIN OSMOND Story

by

Justin Osmond

with

Shirley Bahlmann

Hearing with my Heart: The Justin Osmond Story

Published by Justin Osmond
P.O. Box 282
Ephraim, Utah 84627

www.justinosmond.com

ISBN: 978-0-9830503-0-8

Printed in the United States of America
First Printing 2011

I dedicate this book to my sweet mother.
She is truly the one who inspired me
every day since I was born.
My father was my mentor and motivator,
and my mother was my teacher.

ACKNOWLEDGEMENTS

Although this book is an autobiography, my intent is to recognize and express gratitude to all those who have touched my life in so many ways! Because of you, I can hear with my heart.

First and foremost, I acknowledge my beloved parents for your unconditional love, unwavering support, and for always believing in me! Many miracles were wrought and continue to unfold because of your dedication in helping me be all I can be. There are no words to describe my heartfelt gratitude and true love for what you have done for me. Father, thank you for demonstrating your humility and unconditional love towards me and all humanity. I will always cherish the personal chats, laughs, and tears that we've shared together. Mother, thank you for your daily nourishment and unconquerable spirit in helping me recognize my potential. I thank my Heavenly Father daily for allowing me the privilege and honor of being your son. I couldn't have asked for better parents. Know of my eternal love for you!

I also want to express my appreciation to my siblings. You guys were my best friends growing up and still are to this day. Thank you for your patience and understanding in dealing with my imperfections. You were always there for me when I needed a shoulder to lean on. I hope this book can somehow portray my sincere appreciation and love for all you've done for me.

I would like to personally thank all my dear friends who have accepted me for "who" I am and not "what" I am. I am truly blessed to be surrounded by such amazing friends who have motivated me to be who I am today! It's people like you that make people like me, like people like you!

To all my teachers, speech/language pathologists, audiologists, hearing specialists, thank you for recognizing my potential, believing in my dreams, and never giving up on me!

I would be ungrateful if I didn't recognize all my dear friends at the Starkey Hearing Foundation. Thank you Bill Austin for the amazing opportunities around the world and to be a part of such a wonderful cause. Thank you for providing the "Gift of Better Hearing" to not only myself and my family but to thousands of children worldwide–*So the World May Hear!*

And, of course, Shirley Bahlmann, thank you for your sleepless hours of listening, typing, writing, and editing this book. You truly have a gift that has not only blessed me, but the lives of many. A sincere "thank you" for your support and encouragement along the way.

This book would not be possible if it weren't for the support of many of my kind and generous friends. Thank you for your contribution and generosity.

Lastly, and most importantly, I want to thank my Savior Jesus Christ. He is the one whom I recognize and acknowledge in all of my successes and accomplishments. Despite my weaknesses and shortcomings, He is the one who has lifted me up to greater heights. He is the true source of my joy and happiness. I know that I am nothing, but with Him I can become all that He wants me to be.

– Justin Osmond

ADDITIONAL ENDORSEMENTS

"If you've ever felt like giving up, you need this book. After turning the last page, you'll want to turn it over and read it again. The examples from the life of Justin Osmond show that anything—and I mean anything—is possible."
— Rudy Ruettiger - From the movie "Rudy"

"Justin Osmond has as much courage and dedication as the best athletes that I have scouted for the Steelers."
— Arthur J. Rooney - V.P. of the NFL Pittsburgh Steelers

"I am truly lucky to know Justin Osmond. Whenever he walks into a room, the whole room lights up. His smile is infectious. His heart is so warm, and he is one of the few people I know who is truly genuine to all deaf and hard-of-hearing children and adults. *Hearing with my Heart* is the book to read because it tells you who Justin really is . . . an inspiration to all, as he is to me."
— Marlee Matlin - Deaf Actress

"On Extreme Makeover Home Edition, we were told it couldn't be done, and we did it. Justin Osmond also overcame many Extremes and this book will inspire you to do the same!"
— Herb Ankrom, Producer - ABC's "Extreme Makeover Home Edition" and NBC's "School Pride"

"Justin is the only deaf person I know who truly understands the rhythm of the music and treasures the beauty of the sounds, and yet masters his communication beautifully with deaf and hearing people."
— Heather Whitestone McCallum - Former Miss America; first Miss America with a hearing impairment

"From cover to cover, I am reminded how Justin's challenges have become my blessings. He tackles his world of silence, with the noise that surrounds him, and teaches us the fine art of believing in oneself while balancing challenges with opportunities. This is a remarkable read that's hard to put down. Definitely one of my favorite books!"
— *Ron Clark - Public Relations/Public Affairs Director of Brigham Young University*

"It's a tribute to the soundness of his character, his genuine heart and spirit, that Justin Osmond never leaves you thinking he's missing anything in this life—regardless of his challenges. He's an inspiration, and—I'm proud to say—a friend."
— *Wayne LaPierre - Executive Vice President, National Rifle Association (NRA)*

"As a hearing impaired person and someone who has observed Justin for a number of years, I continue to be amazed and inspired by him. His sense of duty to others, his optimism, his positive approach to everything he does, and the smile permanently formed on his face speak volumes about him. He simply doesn't let anything drag him down. He is happiest and smiling brightest when he helps others— particularly those with hearing disabilities."
— *John Fox - V.P., Royal Caribbean Cruises Ltd.*

"If you've ever said, 'I can't,' I challenge you to pick up this book and see why you can! Justin's ability to overcome extreme challenges proves that anyone can fulfill their dreams. Imagine growing up in a family of famous musicians without being able to hear. But Justin didn't let his deafness slow him down. His story truly motivates us all to make the most of our abilities."
— *Glen Taylor - Owner of Minnesota Timberwolves and Lynx; Chairman & CEO of Taylor Corporation*

"I've had the pleasure of knowing Justin for a number of years now and have worked with him on missions to help impoverished children and adults in Africa and Central America hear through the gift of hearing aids. He is truly a remarkable young man. He connects

immediately with hearing impaired people everywhere because he personally understands the challenges they face, but his compassion, quiet strength, determination and optimism are an inspiration to everyone he meets, regardless of how well they can hear."
— *Randy Raymond - Vice President, Global Hearing Aid Batteries, Rayovac*

"Having been with Justin at missions for children and adults with hearing disabilities, I saw first-hand the caring and empathetic way he involves his heart and mind to deliver support and reassurance. A True Humanitarian."
— *Richard M. Schulze - Founder & Owner, Best Buy*

"The school of hard knocks has taught me that life can be tough— no matter who you are. It takes courage and hard work for the average person to be great. Then there's Justin who goes beyond the norm. Despite his adversities, he has become an inspiration to so many people. If you've ever felt like you've been dealt a bad hand in life and can't succeed, then read this book. You will be inspired by Justin and his undying ability to be optimistic, determined, and successful."
— *Donny Osmond - Singer and entertainer*

"We all love Cinderella stories. They speak to everything human about us. Justin's underdog journey reaches the depths of the soul, and we are winners as we replay his victory on the field of life."
— *Steve Young - NFL Hall of Fame*

"Justin's story is truly inspiring. Discovering what he accomplished with all the challenges he faced in his life made me realize that none of us have to limit ourselves. The next time I hear someone complain that they can't reach their goals, I'm going to hand them a copy of this book."
— *Senator Orrin Hatch - Utah*

"There is more to strength than having big muscles. A strong heart can bring you lasting happiness. My friend Justin shows in his book how to use different kinds of strength and never give up on the things that really matter."
— *Lou Ferrigno - Actor, "The Incredible Hulk"*

x

FOREWORD

My sincere hope is that this story may broaden and enlighten the minds of those who may not quite understand the paradigm thinking of a hearing impaired individual such as myself.

A child's early development is crucial to his upbringing, so imagine my being born into a world void of sound. No comforting sounds of family, friends, and music. No animated sounds from Disney cartoons. No parental sounds of bedtime stories and lullabies. After nearly two years of complete silence, large hardware devices are then strapped to my body and ears. I'm forced out of my quiet comfort zone into an unknown environment of clamor and complexity, unable to sense and understand my surroundings above the hubbub. Thus begins my transition from a world of silence into a discordant world of sounds.

I hope the following personal stories, experiences and thoughts will help create an appreciation of and understanding towards those who live in a world void of sound. Again, I express my utmost appreciation to all who influenced my life in these critical early stages. Because of their help I can now speak with passion, hear with conviction, and sign with animation!

On the flip side, I reach out to all my deaf friends and others who may struggle with hearing loss. I hope you will find comfort and peace in these pages knowing that you are not alone in your challenges. These experiences reflect what God knows about me and about you, and what He offers to help make our weaknesses become our strengths.

Living simultaneously in both the hearing and deaf worlds, I find myself in a unique situation. I have come to accept both the favorable and unfavorable circumstances that inevitably come my way. I may not have a perfect sense of hearing, but deep inside I know I have the capability of hearing with my heart; Helen Keller says it best, "The most beautiful things in the world cannot be seen or even touched, they must be felt with the heart."

In spite of the challenges and obstacles that come our way, I know that if we strive to listen and feel with our hearts–and let that be our true guide–we will experience more joy and happiness in our everyday lives.

May we listen, hear, and understand with not only our physical ears, but our spiritual ears–*our heart.*

–Justin Osmond

"The most beautiful things in this life cannot be seen or heard, but can only be felt in the heart."

— Helen Keller

Chapter 1

Four walls, plus a roof, minus air conditioning, equaled a shirt plastered to my back. I couldn't help wondering if we could have found a more ancient Panamanian building to work in. Reaching around as far as I could, I tried pulling the shirt away from my damp skin, but it didn't help cool me off. I glanced through the torn screen door at broad green jungle leaves waving an invitation to escape under their shade. Although they appeared cool and welcoming, there was no place to escape the thick equatorial humidity. Beads of sweat tickled my hairline. I wiped them away with the back of my hand, but others soon took their place. I thought longingly of the soccer field we'd once used for a hearing mission site. It seemed incredibly primitive at the time, but now I wished to be outside where I might catch any hint of a stray breeze.

In spite of the discomfort, I was grateful to be there. The geographical sites targeted for our philanthropic efforts were as varied as the people who received our hearing aids. Almost all of our humanitarian missions were done in third-world countries with poor facilities, among people who had no hope of hearing without some kind of intervention. If we were fortunate enough to set up in an upscale hotel, it was an exceptionally positive experience for everyone. The delight of sharing the wonders of modern conveniences was almost as good as giving the people we served a trip to Disneyland. After they saw some of the modern marvels of the world, they went home with not only better hearing, but also wondrous memories of running water and electric lights. Many of the people we served considered themselves lucky if they had a one room shack of scrap lumber to live in. The unlucky ones took shelter under cardboard, leaves and branches.

I glanced at the list of patients we'd seen that day, satisfied that all the names were crossed off except the last one—a young boy who was already in the chair. Stretching my back to get the kinks out, I swatted at a pesky fly, then turned to check on the boy's progress. His knobby knees stuck out from beneath the ragged hems of a pair of shorts. His head was tipped sideways, his big brown eyes wide with wonder as the hearing specialist gently fitted a hearing aid into his ear canal. The boy's legs bounced with excitement. His mother reached out a slender brown hand and placed it on one of his knees. The boy stopped bouncing, and his mother withdrew, leaning into her husband who stood just as silently as his wife. They watched with cautious joy until the hearing specialist was done. When she released the boy's head, his eyes widened, and his mouth opened in wonder.

"Mi pequeño?" his mother said with a little catch in her voice.

A boy receives the gift of better hearing

The boy blinked in surprise and let out a yell, which seemed to startle him. He jumped up from his chair as though it had given him a shock. Running to his mother, he wrapped his arms around her waist. His father put a loving hand on the boy's hair. He bent his head for a moment, then turned to look at us, his eyes made even darker by unshed tears. "Gracias," he said, blinking rapidly. "Muchas gracias."

In spite of the heat and fatigue, my joy swelled as I watched the boy touch his new hearing aids with gentle, curious fingers. When the family left and the door banged behind them, the boy jumped and clutched his mother's hand. Then they were gone. I silently wished him well on his journey in a whole new world of sound.

I was more than ready to pack up and return to my room. I wanted to take out my own hearing aids and sink into the silence that only deafness can offer. I looked forward to a night of blissfully undisturbed sleep. But before I could open a single case to pack our equipment, the door opened. I turned to see a very old woman coming through the doorway with eyes sunken into a dark face full of wrinkles. Two younger women supported her on either side. One of them stepped forward and raised her voice in urgent Spanish. Our international mission director, Frederic Rondeau, and I gave up packing our equipment long enough to listen. I dragged a chair closer so the old woman could sit down. Her companions lowered her into it.

Frederic asked questions in Spanish. I know a little Spanish, and I knew this elderly woman was not on our list. It was common for people to find out about our hearing missions after we arrived, so we always packed extra hearing aids. It would be no problem to fit her if she was a candidate. Bill Austin, owner and founder of The Starkey Hearing Foundation, joined the discussion. I couldn't even understand the English portions of the conversation with so many people speaking at once, so I just waited. After a few moments Bill turned his intense gaze on me. "Justin," he said.

I faced him, reading his lips as he spoke.

"We have a candidate here in her nineties who needs hearing aids. What do you think of making some insta-molds for this lovely young lady?"

I glanced at the woman in the chair, then turned back to Bill and responded, "I'm on it!"

Bill raised a hand and rubbed his chin. "Just a minute. There's a problem."

"Not her age," I protested. "We once fitted a 113-year-old lady in Michigan."

"It's not that," Bill replied. "This woman is terminally ill. The doctors diagnosed her with two months left to live."

Two months? My heart lurched as I tried to imagine what it would be like to have my life measured in such a short increment of time.

Bill rubbed his furrowed brow with a knuckle. "She desperately wants to hear her grandchildren laugh before she dies. What do you think? Is it worth giving her hearing aids if she only has two months to live?"

My life flashed before me. I watched my father singing the lead for the Osmonds in the Wembley Stadium of London, England; I was together with my family at Christmas, laughing, singing, and conversing; I was listening at church, striving to understand what my Heavenly Father would have me do; I could hear my nieces and nephews yelling, "Uncle Justy!"; I was rocked to sleep hearing my mother's angelic voice singing me bedtime tunes; I heard my brother Travis tell me on the radio/walkie-talkie during a deer hunt, "Justin, There's a big buck coming right at ya!" Then I remembered my Grandmother, Olive Osmond's, dying words. "Justin, you will play a mighty role in the deaf community. Don't ever give up on them!"

I turned to Bill and replied with no hesitation, "Yes! Absolutely yes!"

Bill grinned. "Then what are we waiting for? Let's bring laughter to her ears!"

"If you fear failure, then you do not have the faith sufficient enough to believe that God will lead you to your final destiny."
— Merrill Osmond

Chapter 2

Merrill and Mary Osmond welcomed me into their household on March 1, 1977. If there had been routine screenings for hearing loss back then, my life may have taken a different turn. As it was, my parents bundled me up and took me home from the hospital with no idea that I was deaf.

My seventeen-month-old brother Travis thought I was an interesting new addition to the family. As Mother watched us grow together, she soon observed that I was not progressing the same way Travis had. For one thing, I didn't respond to her voice when she came to get me from my nap. I only smiled when I saw her, then waved my arms for her to pick me up. Mother took me to several doctors who all basically told her that once my frequent ear infections cleared up, I'd be fine. Over the course of a year, I learned how to hold my bottle, walk on my own, and throw tantrums whenever I wanted something. I didn't even try to say words. I just yelled at the top of my voice until my mother guessed what I wanted. It was usually something simple, like a glass of chocolate milk, but I didn't know how to tell her that.

When I was eighteen months old, Travis and I were playing in our back yard when Mother opened the door and called us to come into the house. Travis obediently headed toward her, but I kept on playing because I didn't see Travis leave. If I'd seen him, I'm sure I would have followed as I usually did. Mother stood in the doorway for a moment, watching me, her worst fears crowding to the surface. Suddenly, she determined that she would no longer accept pat assurances that I was fine. She made an appointment with an audiologist at Brigham Young University (BYU). After evaluating the tests, the audiologist called my mother with the heartbreaking news, "Your son has a hearing problem." At last, someone else recognized what Mother already knew in her heart. Even though she'd suspected it all along, the first thing she did was cry.

Sixty percent of hearing loss is genetic, so I jokingly blame my uncles, Tom and Virl, for my condition. Virl, Tom, and I each have about 90% hearing loss in both ears. Our losses are on slightly different frequencies, but they're basically the same. The only other family member I know who's been affected by this genetic hearing loss is Father's cousin, Tracy Miller. We're all in this together.

In reality, Virl and Tom are my heroes. I imagine them watching from backstage and behind the scenes while their brothers and sister achieved world fame. Virl and Tom could have been bitter, but they chose to be better, and that has made all the difference in the world—to themselves and everyone around them.

George, Tom, Justin, and Virl Osmond
demonstrating sign language for "I Love You"

I've experienced similar feelings of frustration as the son of Merrill, the world-renowned lead singer of the Osmonds, who sold more gold and platinum records than the Beatles and the Jackson Five in one year. The Osmonds also broke records for sellout performances once held by the Beatles and Elvis Presley. Imagine your father and uncles singing their hearts out to a maximum capacity crowd in Wembley Stadium, London, with crowds of screaming fans, flashing lights, sequins sparkling and fringe swaying as their top hits rang out over the sound system. I could hear the music, but couldn't understand the words. My memories are very clear. It was the strangest thing because in the middle of a crowd, I felt like I was standing alone. It's one of the worst feelings in the world.

Travis and Merrill sing, while Justin tries to read Merrill's lips to figure out what song they're singing

"Closeness is a matter of communication; communication is a matter of understanding; understanding is a matter of being able to hear."

— Anonymous

Chapter 3

Can you imagine life without sound? Never hearing the comforting voices of loved ones, cheering fans at sports events, or "Auld Lang Syne" at New Year's Eve? Imagine watching people's lips move, but not hearing or understanding a single word they say. Try turning the sound off the television and watch it for a while to see if you can figure out what's going on.

That is my life without hearing aids.

Everyone has some form of adversity, but in spite of trials, everyone should be allowed the chance to grow and achieve everything they possibly can. Having a hearing loss shouldn't stop people from being who they really are. If it's too hard to be understood, they may feel it's easier to give up trying. Isolation follows; then their family and friends may stop trying to communicate with them.

Since I was born deaf, I've had the opportunity to start life's journey on a rather unique path. I know what it's like to grow up in an environment as foreign to hearing people as palm trees are to polar bears.

Human needs can be summed up in a profound and simple phrase: we all want to be understood. A close second is the desire to reach our aspirations in life. One of my aspirations is to help motivate people to reach their heart's desire. A key element in achievement is good, clear communication. If you want to communicate with someone, you'll obviously have to understand one another.

I thought it was ironic when I was invited to be the keynote speaker at a cellular phone convention. I was flattered, even though my first thought was, "Why me? How can a person who can't hear effectively use the phone?" It's true that current technology makes it possible, but it's still not easy. If you want to draw closer to someone and build trust, you need to communicate, because that is a large part of what makes us human. In order to communicate, you need to understand, and the easiest way to understand is with speech and hearing. When that becomes a challenge, the alternate form of communication is sign language.

It's hard to imagine communicating with someone who is both blind and deaf. Helen Keller was an exceptional example of overcoming daunting trials. Born with perfectly normal senses, she became so gravely ill as a toddler that her parents feared for her life. They were delighted when she recovered, but they soon learned that cheating death cost Helen both sight and hearing. The bewildered Kellers didn't even consider education for their handicapped child. How could she possibly be taught? Not knowing what else to do, they allowed her to run wild. She grabbed food off people's plates and threw fits when she didn't get what she wanted. It was the only method she knew for communicating.

The gifted Anne Sullivan took on the seemingly impossible task of educating Helen. With her teacher's patience and a firm hand, Helen eventually learned to communicate in a way that others could understand. Anne used sign language by forming the letters with her hand in Helen's palm. Once people could get through to Helen, someone asked the thought-provoking question, "If you had to choose between being blind or deaf, which would you choose?"

This seems like an easy answer. I know for myself that I was terrified of the dark as a child. When I conducted my own straw poll, I found that 99% of people I surveyed said they'd rather be deaf than blind. Helen Keller's answer was as unexpected as it is profound. "I am just as deaf as I am blind," she said. "The problems of deafness are deeper and more complex, if not more important, than those of blindness. Deafness is a much worse misfortune, for it means the loss of the most vital stimulus—the sound of the voice that brings language, sets thoughts astir, and keeps us in the intellectual company of man." In other words, blindness separates people from things, but deafness separates people from people.

In the 1950s, Grandma Olive Osmond, matriarch of the musical family, faced a heart-breaking situation when her two oldest sons, Virl and Tom, were born deaf. In the mid-1900s, there weren't a lot of resources available for children with hearing loss. Some of the hearing aids were still made with a small tube stuck in the ear and the other end shaped like a hearing trumpet. Grandma Olive didn't sit around feeling sorry. She took action and formed The Osmond Foundation, which helped not only her sons, but many others as it promoted hearing health awareness on a sustained scale. As the organization grew, it was renamed The Children's Miracle Network. Today, The Children's Miracle Network is the largest telethon in the world, raising funds to help children with a wide variety of medical diagnoses.

When the Osmond's third son, Alan, was born, he was found with not only excellent hearing, but an affinity for music. He was followed by his equally musical brothers Wayne, Merrill, Jay, Donny, and Jimmy. Grandma, an accomplished saxophone player, enrolled her sons in music lessons. They began with the saxophone, which later evolved into guitars, drums, and keyboards. Grandpa George got them started with vocals by singing along in the car to barbershop quartet tunes such as "The Old Oaken Bucket."

Although rich in boys (the only daughter, Marie, was born between brothers Donny and Jimmy), my grandparents were not the most financially well-to-do couple in Ogden, Utah. They desperately wanted Virl and Tom to have the best hearing aids available. Just about all of Grandpa's paycheck went toward providing a living for his growing family, and hearing aids weren't cheap. Yet as the boys became more involved in music, their parents realized they had a unique opportunity. Their very gifted sons performed at local talent shows, community concerts, and church activities. They were born entertainers, and the more they sang, the more they wanted to perform.

That's when the family decided to use the other boys' talents to help Virl and Tom. They would pool their performance money to buy the best hearing aids on the market. With a clear goal in mind, Grandpa's

World War II army sergeant skills came in handy in organizing the boys and their musical events. He booked the Osmonds for performances wherever he could, from local county fair rodeos to boxing matches.

In 1958 when my father, Merrill, was six years old, the family garnered an audition for the Lawrence Welk Show in California. It was a thrilling opportunity. Grandpa George tied the luggage on top of the station wagon and the family climbed in. It was a long drive across the barren state of Nevada to reach California. The family sang along the way, practicing their audition number and several others just for the fun of it. The closer they got to Los Angeles, the more excited they became. This could be their big break. If all went well, they would have enough money to buy new hearing aids for Virl and Tom.

At last they stared out the windows in wonder at tall buildings and exotic palm trees lining the wide streets of the "City of Angels." The temperature was a balmy seventy-four degrees. The family pulled up to a budget motel and burst out of the car, anxious to be on their feet again. The bigger boys helped carry in the luggage, ready and eager to go onstage with their best performance ever. That's when they got the heart-breaking phone message from a representative of the Lawrence Welk Show. "I'm sorry, but we are simply unable to put you on the show. We're canceling your audition."

I can only imagine what my father and uncles felt. It may have been worse for Grandma and Grandpa, since they had to haul their family such a long way only to have their dream snatched from them at the last minute.

Instead of giving in to discouragement, Grandpa turned to his disappointed sons and said, "Don't let this get you down, boys. We're going to Disneyland and have some fun before we head home." You have to admire the fact that even though his children had missed a golden opportunity, Grandpa made a real effort to keep them in good spirits and make the situation more positive.

It's interesting to note that not only did the Osmonds have a strong family resemblance, but they also had a tradition of dressing alike. Grandma Olive's home sewn shirts made her children stand out in a crowd, making it less likely she would lose one. That's why all her boys wore their matching audition outfits to Disneyland. Rides weren't the only attraction there. Open pavilions housed live bands playing peppy numbers, as well as singers belting out crowd-pleasing tunes. The Osmond family stopped at one pavilion that featured a barbershop quartet called "The Dapper Dans." This was particularly appealing, since four-part harmony was the Osmonds claim to fame, so they stopped to listen. The Dapper Dans couldn't help noticing the boys in matching outfits standing on the front row. On impulse, one of the quartet members called out, "Hey, you all look alike. I'll bet you do something. Is it singing or dancing?"

"We can sing," answered ten-year-old Alan.

"Well then, why don't you come up here and sing a song for us?" the man asked.

So Alan, Wayne, Merrill, and Jay climbed on stage. They stood shoulder to shoulder, and without a hint of bashfulness, sang out in perfect four-part harmony. The audience was so amazed at the pint-sized singers' talent that they called out, "Yeah! That was great! Do another one!" So the Osmonds sang another, then another, while the audience nudged each other and whispered, "They've got talent!" and "They're good!" The Osmonds made such an impact that the Dapper Dans tracked down Walt Disney and told him, "There's a very unique group of little boys out there with amazing voices."

Walt Disney said, "All right, bring them in." When the Osmonds came into the office, Disney said, "I hear you guys have talent. Sing something for me." So they did. Disney was so impressed that he opened the door of opportunity, giving the Osmonds their big break into the entertainment world.

This just goes to show that all things are possible, even when they seem impossible. Think about what might have happened if the Osmonds had made the audition and performed on the Lawrence Welk Show. That would have been a whole different audience. What if Grandpa had turned around and taken his family home immediately after the cancelled audition news? A lot of things could have happened differently, but they didn't. What are the chances that a family vacation would lead to the defining moment of meeting Walt Disney? When we least expect it, divine intervention has a way of pointing us in the right direction.

With brotherly love as their driving force, the young quartet grew to become one of the most popular singing groups in the 20th Century. It was almost like divine intervention, being in the right place at the right time. But for whatever reason, the family soon found themselves in a financial position to obtain the best hearing aids available for Virl and Tom, so they wouldn't have to live in a world of silence.

"Real character is shown after the emotion of the moment has gone."

– Jeffrey R. Holland

Chapter 4

My diagnosis shocked everyone in the extended Osmond family, including my father. He hadn't suspected a thing. This was understandable because he wasn't around me as much as my mother. He thought I was a funny little guy who always kept everyone laughing, so what could be wrong? Even when Father found out, he adjusted a little more easily than Mother, most likely because of growing up with Virl and Tom. In spite of his experience, the situation jarred both my parents. They couldn't help wondering if they had done something wrong. Was there any way they could have prevented this from happening? They even asked themselves why, out of all the Osmonds, was I the only one who inherited the deaf gene?

There were no clear answers, so after drying their eyes, my parents asked themselves what they could possibly do to make my situation better. Virl and Tom both knew sign language—an efficient form of communication for the deaf—but Mother didn't want that for me. She remembered a time when she had to help Virl order food at a restaurant and help him get a plane ticket. The bulk of childcare naturally fell on Mother's shoulders, and she was determined not to let anything like that happen to me. "We need to get him into some good speech therapy programs," she told Father. She made it clear that her goal was to have me function as normally as possible. They both agreed on the importance of speech development in my childhood, so they got me into speech, listening, and comprehension therapy as soon as possible, with Mother vowing to stuff as much speech into me as I could hold.

Teaching speech to a one-and-a-half-year-old child, who had never heard sound, would take a lot of work—not only for me, but my parents as well. They made a commitment to do all they could in order to help me succeed. Even if they had known how much mental and physical exertion they were in for, I'm certain they would still have agreed to do it. They flew me all over the country to meet with doctors and hearing specialists, searching far and wide for the best programs available. My parents finally chose world-renowned otolaryngologist (ear, nose, and throat, or ENT) specialist Doctor John House in Los Angeles to perform exploratory surgery. His findings ruled out conductive hearing loss—a treatable condition by fixing any missing or malfunctioning ear bones. Unfortunately, mine was a sensorial neural hearing loss, which is an untreatable genetic nerve deafness. I had pulled the hereditary gene from the cosmic gene pool.

Hearing loss functions are labeled Normal, Mild, Moderate, Severe, and Profound. With a 90% loss, mine couldn't get much worse, and I was placed in the Severe to Profound category.

With this diagnosis came another important decision. Which method was best to help me hear as much as possible? I was a prime candidate for a cochlear implant, which required a very intensive surgical procedure. A patch of hair must be shaved behind the recipient's ear, then a hole is cut through the skull to insert the internal components of the receiver. An electrode system is carefully run through the inner ear and into the cochlea. These internal electrodes collect impulses from a stimulator and send them to different regions of the auditory nerve.

The outer components of the cochlear implant consist of a small transmitter system on the outside of the skull. This receives signals from a speech processor and converts them to electric impulses. There is also a sound processor, which selects and arranges sounds picked up by a small microphone tucked behind the ear. An implant does not fully restore normal hearing, but provides a useful representation of sound which must then be interpreted by the listener, usually with the help of speech therapy.

Because of the complex electrode array inserted into the cochlea, implants are a one-shot deal. It can't be taken out and tried again. Even though the failure rate is low, if it doesn't work, it's too late. Besides that, any surgical procedure is risky—especially on an eighteen-month-old. A lot of doctors tried to convince my parents to give me a cochlear implant, assuring them it was the best option for me. Their professional argument was, "The earlier we can get him on an implant, the earlier he will hear and speak."

Obviously I couldn't make a decision like that for myself, so my parents carefully weighed the pros and cons and made the choice for me. They decided they didn't want to take the surgical risk until they'd tried every other option available.

Cochlear implants are a miracle for those who have hardly any residual hearing. A lot of my close friends have benefited from implants and are happy with them. With advances in the medical field, today's implants are safer and more secure than they were when I was eighteen months old. I'm supportive of that step, but I encourage researching all possible options before making any decision.

To this day, I'm grateful that my parents chose traditional hearing aids for me. Their belief in technological advances proved true. In fact, I like to see people smile when I say that I can now hear so well, I can hear what people are thinking—and they usually think I'm crazy!

Seriously though, test results have convinced me that my current hearing aids provide the best hearing I can possibly get. I also credit my hearing ability to long hours of therapy, training, practice, and my parents teaching me to believe in myself. Whether you believe you can, or believe you can't, you're right!

"You may have tangible wealth untold, caskets of jewels and coffers of gold, but richer than I you can never be—I had a mother who read to me."

– Stricklan Gillilan

Chapter 5

The moment a hearing person is born, they begin picking up voices and sounds all around them. Since people model what they hear, it stands to reason that this sensory input develops their individual speech patterns. This is evident in the dialects heard all across the United States, from a southern drawl to a northeasterner's dropped consonants to a Midwesterner's clipped words. On paper, what they're saying reads the same, but the oral presentation is noticeably different—proving that children's speech development is influenced by hearing role models. So when someone comes across an unfamiliar accent, or even an unaccustomed pitch of voice, communication is more difficult for the listener.

At a young age, I experienced another awkward incident that was inevitable for someone like me. I never intended to make an enemy at a water park. I just wanted to have fun with my family. One of the coolest features at the park was a Jacuzzi hot tub big enough for a child like me to swim in. So I cinched on my swimming goggles and paddled across the expanse of warm water. Air jets blasted out bubbles like a magical fairy tale pool.

Before long, I noticed a lifeguard following my progress along the side of the pool. Glancing up, I noticed him facing my direction. His beard bobbed up and down, making me wonder if he was chewing bubble gum. He didn't have a belly that shook like jelly, but he did have a beard that looked short and weird. With water in my goggles and no hearing aids in, I couldn't figure out exactly what he was doing. Was he saying something? He must have been trying to get someone else's attention, because I wasn't doing anything wrong. I was just swimming in a water park. *Hello?* You're supposed to swim here! But Santa kept pace with me while I kept paddling. I glanced around, but everyone else in the hot tub was settled around the edges, watching me. I kept going, wishing with each passing second that Santa Claus would leave this Caribbean paradise and go back to the North Pole where he belonged.

At last I reached the far side of the pool. There he was, his big arms reaching down to haul me out of the water, his angry eyes glaring at me over his beard. He began chewing away inside that mass of hair. I suspected he was yelling at me, but he could have been speaking Portuguese for all the good his shouting did. If he wanted me to have any chance of reading his lips, he'd have to shave first.

My mother rushed to my rescue, explaining that I was deaf. When he finally learned I wasn't really on the naughty list, he calmed down and returned to his sleigh. Mother told me there was no swimming allowed in the hot tub. The lifeguard had given me three warnings and was ready to banish me from the pool.

Besides beards, another difficulty for me has been sounds beyond my range of hearing—especially when everyone else around can hear them. A recurring problem throughout life has been the inability to hear frequencies as high as, say, a referee's whistle.

One memorable event occurred when my team qualified for the soccer playoffs. We were excited, ready to pound down the field with our whole heart and soul. We ended up playing so well that we tied the game with just a few precious minutes left. I was playing the position of mid-field halfback. As I got in position, I was keenly aware of the ticking clock and focused my total attention on the task of making just one more goal. I wanted to score so badly that I felt if I could just get the ball, nothing could stop me.

Then, miracle of miracles, the ball rolled toward me. I began dribbling it towards the goal net. Sweat trickled down my back as I made a quick pass to one of my teammates. Trotting down the edge of the field, I kept my eyes on the ball and was ready when it passed right back to me. Time was running out. The window of opportunity was closing with every second that passed. I set my jaw, determined to put that ball in the net.

I flew down the field with the ball, barely noticing the other players slowing down until it was just me and the goalie. I kicked that ball for all I was worth. Watching its progress with breathless anticipation, I wondered for a split second if it was going to miss the goal. When I saw it zip past the goalie and tuck itself into the corner of the net, I was ecstatic. Yes! I jumped up and down in a joyous dance of victory. We won! We won! I spun around, my hands pumping the air half a dozen times before I realized that my team was not celebrating with me. What was wrong with them? We'd just won the game!

I stopped and glanced at the surrounding faces, fixed with looks of incredulity, and a prickle of embarrassment crawled down my neck. What was going on? I glanced at the referee, who frowned and gestured in my direction with the whistle poised at his mouth. It didn't take me long to figure out that the referee had been blowing his whistle because I was offside when I took that last pass. The hard-won goal didn't count.

The question for me is, should I occasionally stop and look around to see if the whistle's blowing, or should I be proactive and keep playing with the risk of shooting a worthless goal? Even though I can't hear the whistle, if I check the referees often enough, I may see them blowing on it. In the meantime, I may lose an opportunity to help my team win. I figure it's best to just keep playing.

That's what we all have to do. Don't hold back. Take the information you know and give it your best shot without looking back.

One time I was really in the zone, and it seemed that no one could get my attention to let me know the whistle blew. The referee was so frustrated by my actions that he gave me a yellow card, which is a penalty—a major warning that if you don't start playing by the protocols of the game, you'll be ejected. If you get two yellow cards you're out of the game. I took my penalty card without explaining anything to the referee. I didn't want to make a big deal out of not being able to hear the whistle because I felt like I was just one of the other kids.

Ears are a very obvious part of our anatomy, yet they do not do the actual hearing. Ear canals are open channels for sound waves to travel through, transporting sound waves into the brain for interpretation. It is remarkable that this process is the result of physical movement with no chemical reactions involved.

Sound vibrates the atmosphere, using outward moving particles to carry the vibrational pulse through the air. Different frequencies make different sounds. The cup-shaped outer ear not only captures sound waves, but also helps determine from which direction they originate. The waves travel down the ear canal and hit the eardrum, which compresses to move the smallest bones in the human body: the malleus (commonly known as the hammer), the incus (commonly referred to as the anvil), and the stapes, or stirrup. This chain reaction causes the stapes to act as a piston against the fluid-filled cochlea—an action necessary to drive sound waves through the thick fluid. The inner ear translates the faithfully duplicated sound waves into nerve pulses the brain can understand. This is how we hear with our brain, not our ears.

Since hearing is obviously difficult for a person who is deaf, a lot of doctors tried convincing my parents that I should learn American Sign Language (ASL). Others tried persuading them to teach me to speak, while others tried to talk them into letting me become skilled at both. Partly because I come from a musical family, when presented with the options of speech or signing, my parents chose to concentrate exclusively on hearing and speech. The reality is that if you can talk, you can function better in a hearing society. My mother was so determined to have me speak that when Uncle Tom sat me on the counter and started teaching me to sign, she chased him out of the house. "As soon as Justin knows all the speech he can, then he may learn to sign. But until he's sixteen, he's only going to learn speech," she declared. That was a daring statement.

With the diagnosis of severe to profound hearing loss attached to me for life, I had to work overtime to catch up with my hearing peers. Well-meaning people who thought that speaking to me with exaggerated mouth movements would help me learn to talk were actually no help at all. Instead of being impressed, I would laugh at their comically exaggerated mouths. I couldn't help it. They were acting funny instead of giving me an accurate model to copy. If anything, the antics from their belief that I was completely impaired made things worse. How can you read lips when they're being stretched in fantastic, crazy formations like elastic bands? The best thing to do while communicating with a hearing impaired person is to simply speak the way you would to a hearing person.

Of course, hearing aids were necessary in order for me to hear enough speech to mimic, but try pushing a couple of cold, hard molds into an eighteen-month-old's ear canals while hooking them behind his ears and see what happens. I hated them. Not only did they feel strange, but I was so used to silence that the sudden world of sound was terrifying. It takes awhile for the brain to become accustomed to sounds it's never heard. Even now, when I get an upgraded hearing device with better technology, I hear things I've never heard before. Recently, when I got my new Starkey hearing aids, I was driving my car and signaled a left turn. That was when I heard the ticking of the turn signal for the first time in my life. At first it was annoying; then I realized it was a normal sound, and I grew accustomed to it.

Back when I was a year and a half old, it was a real battle for my mother to make me keep my hearing aids in. She tried everything she could think of, including charts with little boxes I could check off for leaving my hearing aids in for five minutes. The check marks would bring me little prizes or goodies. She also tried pulling a ski cap over my head to cover my ears so I couldn't get to the hearing aids and pull them out. When that didn't work, she put a more rigid bike helmet on me. But no matter what she tried, as soon as I got around the corner and out of her sight, I'd get rid of the headgear and take out my hearing aids. One time, in a desperate moment, she actually duct taped them in. I still managed to remove the hearing aids. When I did, I'd hide them everywhere. I buried them under plants, pushed them into the toes of shoes in my closet, and even flushed them down the toilet. These actions really made my parents upset, and at times, angry. To this day they don't know that I once fed my dog a new pair of hearing aids. This book reveals a secret my parents never knew before, so I hope they can find it in their hearts to forgive me.

When I finally learned to leave my hearing aids in for half an hour at a time, I began to think that it was kind of neat to hear things all around me. By then I was nearly two years old and growing fast.

This meant my hearing aids only fit tightly in my ear canal for about three months, and when they didn't, they emitted annoying squeals. This bothered Mother to the point that she finally learned to make hearing aid molds herself. Whenever I outgrew my hearing aids, my mother would mold me some new ear inserts so she wouldn't have to listen to the high-pitched squeals. I didn't know what all the fuss was about, because the squeals never registered in my hearing range.

With my hearing aids finally being left in, we traveled the country looking for the best speech pathologist available. My first therapist was Carol Keltsch. She was very patient and managed to coax the first verbalized sound out of me by blowing bubbles. My very first recognizable words were "Buh-buh-buh-bubbles."

Mother was delighted. At three years old, she started me on a schedule that grew with me until it eventually included waking up at 5:30 a.m. along with my siblings to begin our day with thirty minutes of family scripture study and prayer. Then I would do thirty minutes of personal speech therapy with Mother, then violin practice for thirty minutes, then piano for thirty more minutes. After a full day of school, I'd go home and read on my own for 30 minutes. After I got my chores and homework done, I could then play with friends.

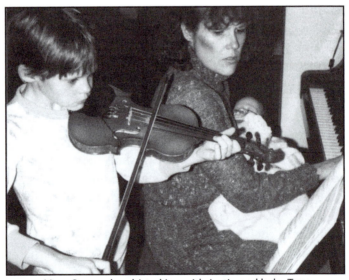

Mary Osmond multi-tasking with Justin and baby Troy

In the evening Mother would sing me some tunes and read me a bedtime story. Last of all, I would read my scriptures before I went to bed. That's a lot of reading in one day, but as I look back I'm grateful my parents had me on such an intense schedule.

A person's spoken language is typically transferred to reading, which makes it crucial to hearing therapy—which is why Mother insisted I do so much of it. Without spoken language to support reading, there is not as much success because it comes across as just a word. The reader is left wondering, *What does it really mean?*

I love the quote by Abraham Lincoln, "All that I am and all that I've become I owe to my mother." And I completely agree. I owe my current achievement and success to my sweet mother! If more mothers would read to their children more often, we would be facing fewer academic and social problems in this nation.

Most children go to school for five or six hours a day with teachers as their mentors. At the end of kindergarten, a child has been in school a total of 700 hours. Politicians are quick to insist that an awful lot of learning had better take place in those hours. If it doesn't, they hold teachers accountable.

On the other hand, children are home for eighteen hours a day. The same child at the end of kindergarten has been outside of school

Justin goes over a boy's new hearing aids

for 52,000 hours. So here's the question: Which teacher has a better chance of influencing his or her child? The classroom teacher who logged in 700 hours or the teachers at home (parents, grandparents, aunts, uncles or nanny) who had the child for 52,000 hours?

No contest.

What a child sees and hears is impressed on their minds. They learn by the models of behavior they see all around them.

Who are our real teachers? My mother stuck with me every single day and never, ever gave up on me. Miracles can happen when people never give up.

*"We never know how high we are 'til we are called to rise,
and then if we are true to plan, our statures will touch the skies."*
– Emily Dickinson

Chapter 6

Mother researched all sources available regarding hearing health awareness without the convenience of the Internet. She even completed highly recommended programs such as the Alexander Graham Bell Association and the John Tracy Clinic courses by mail in order to find more ways to help me.

The original plan was for me to get my education through the School for the Deaf in Ogden, Utah. Mother understood that it was an oral program, but her observations showed it wasn't what she was looking for. Instead she enrolled me in a regular preschool. The president of the School for the Deaf told her, "You're making the biggest mistake of your life." His comment made Mother pause to wonder if she really was wrong to pull me out. After all, the school was staffed with experts who had years of accumulated training and experience with the hearing impaired. What did she know about it? She knew Virl and Tom, but she'd never tried teaching them how to function in a hearing world. In spite of her misgivings, she felt it was the right thing to do, and Father supported her decision.

Now my parents faced a dilemma. Where could I learn to live in a world of speech? The Listen Foundation, the oldest non-profit organization that supports the Acoupedic/Auditory-Verbal teaching philosophy, sent my parents to Doreen Pollack, a trained speech therapist native to Great Britain.

After working on innovative ways to help her deaf nephew learn to communicate, Doreen met her American husband during World War II and made her new home with him in Denver, Colorado. Ironically, the war proved to be a catalyst that furthered Doreen's work. Technology that invented miniature wartime radio transistors could be adapted to create more powerful hearing aids.

While assimilating into the American culture, Doreen continued work with children who were deaf, finding ways to improve on the standard teaching of the time. The break-through program Doreen developed challenged the common method of utilizing an abundance of visual information to teach students with hearing loss. Doreen believed that children with hearing impairment could be trained to listen and become five-sensed citizens through a program called "Auditory-Verbal." This program emphasizes the thinking process through activities, games, and songs. Every day that a student participates in the activities is a crucial step toward integrating them into the hearing world. A strong coach—usually a parent who is guided by the therapist—is key to success.

After forty years, this program still creates a strong demand throughout the world. My parents were delighted with the concept and got me involved right away. My first instruction came straight from Doreen. Since she was close to retirement, she soon turned us over to her protégé, Nancy Calaffe-Schenk, an Auditory-Verbal therapist, audiologist, and teacher of the deaf. Well qualified in her field, Nancy actually helped Doreen write a textbook about this innovative approach.

The individualized program consisted of one-hour sessions each week with the therapist, child, and the parent who spent the most time with the child. Training was given on incorporating listening as a way of life. Nancy basically drew my family a road map outlining the work I was to do for the coming week, the next three months, and the next year. I had three hours a day of intensive therapy working with Nancy; then we'd go back home for a few months, work hard on my listening and speech, then return to Denver for further detailed steps.

Ultimately, every significant person in my life was involved at some level of training, including my nannies, my brothers and sisters, and my parents. My early, intensive training made listening a part of my life. Sometimes it's a challenge, but I can hear and communicate over the phone. I no longer have to think intensely about it, because listening has simply become part of who I am. This early intervention also helped me develop a natural-sounding voice.

Time proved that Mother was not crazy to pull me out of the School for the Deaf. Years later, we ran into the Ogden school's president. He saw for himself the ability I had to speak the words I'd learned.

Another important aspect of my training was mainstreaming with hearing children. After Mother enrolled me in a normal preschool, she got the idea of starting her own school to help preschoolers with hearing impairments. She followed through on her idea, naming her school, "A Child Shall Speak." Although it was begun mainly to help me, it was for all children. Those who needed hearing instruction received the best therapeutic sessions available at the time, including the hearing and speaking therapy training we received from Nancy. This was critical to development. Mainstreaming broke down barriers and built confidence, helping us believe that we could effectively associate with the hearing kids. We learned to associate together. I found out quickly that we weren't really that much different. No one's better than anyone else. We all fit in. We felt like we were all on the same team, and that was a very good feeling indeed.

"To do today's work well and not to bother about tomorrow is the secret of accomplishment"

– William Ostler

Chapter 7

After a year of traveling back and forth to Denver, my parents came up with a bold new plan. In 1982, they invited Nancy to the Sundance Resort restaurant. During the meal, they said, "Nancy, we'd like you to spend more time in Utah working with Justin. What can we do to get you here?"

Nancy was already impressed with my parents' diligence in completing daily speech therapy assignments. She decided that she wanted to do whatever she could to help further my speech development. Her love and regard for my family were all it took for her to accept the job offer and relocate.

One night, a big snowstorm hit. Nancy answered her phone early the next morning to find my mother on the line. "There's so much snow," Mother said. "All the kids are going out to play. Is it all right if I let Justin go out to play instead of doing his therapy this morning?"

Nancy laughed. "Certainly," she replied. "Just have him come in afterward and tell you a story about being in the snow." At that time, my speech wasn't very good, but Nancy's willingness to let me play for one special day instead of repeating vocal exercises proved that she had a heart, even though she was a stickler during therapy.

Perhaps her intensity of purpose and insistence that I toe the line came from the fact that she saw great potential in me. She remembers me as joyful, attentive, gracious, and always prepared for therapy. I admit that I had a craving to learn. I loved to listen and talk, but I would often rather do other things than speech and listening therapy. At times it seemed such a chore, especially since my parents made sure the bulk of my waking hours were spent listening, talking, and learning new vocabulary. It wasn't easy for any of us. But from the current vantage point in my life, I realize how lucky I was to have such intense experiences during childhood. My two uncles didn't have that crucial option when they were younger, so communication in general is more difficult for them as adults.

Two or three times a week the students with hearing impairments were taken out of our pre-school class for speech therapy. Our parents were given a specific assignment, such as a letter of the alphabet that we had to memorize for the week. If we didn't, our parents had to explain the reason why.

When Nancy noticed my love of music—which probably originated from Mother singing to me at night—Nancy made the observation that music is of great benefit in boosting listening skills. Music also helps develop a natural-sounding voice, as well as the ability to remember longer phrases because of the way the lyrics are put together.

Mother was very thoughtful about correcting my speech in public. One of the hardest sounds for me to make is a hard "ch." Since Mother didn't want to call attention to me if I mispronounced a word in public, she made up a silent signal. For example, if she heard me say, "shicken" instead of "chicken," she would catch my eye and lay two fingers along her right cheek while resting her chin in her palm. As soon as I saw that signal, I knew I'd mispronounced a word. No one else knew our system, so I could say, "Oh, excuse me, I mean 'chicken,'" and no one would be the wiser. I really appreciate her concern for my feelings and her ingenuity in figuring out a way to save me from needless embarrassment.

There were so many days when I just wanted to throw speech therapy out the window, it's a wonder Mother wouldn't let me. True to her word, she kept stuffing speech down me. She didn't even let up during vacation. Instead, she enlisted the whole family. This is where Nancy's training for my brothers and sisters paid off. They would play listening games and do speech activities with me while we were on the road. I mostly worked with my brothers Travis and Shane, but I interacted with everyone, which was a great help because they treated me like a normal hearing kid.

After Nancy spent a year in Utah, she accepted a marriage proposal that took her back to Colorado. In that year, she trained a local woman with the necessary skills to keep the Auditory-Verbal program going. Still, no one could completely replace Nancy. Today I occasionally see her at national conventions and tradeshows. At a recent event in Colorado where I was the keynote speaker, I played a song on my violin and dedicated it to Nancy in appreciation for the crucial role she had played in my young life. I thank her for helping me learn to speak with passion and hear with conviction. She saw me from the very first as a child with hearing loss who had every ability, capability, and potential to do and be anything my heart desired. With her move back to Colorado, "A Child Shall Speak" ended.

"If we can learn to turn down our physical hearing and turn up the volume of our spiritual senses, we will hear the music of our hearts. We will hear God's love through the warm sun's rays, the cool breeze through the wind, and the twinkling lights of the stars."

— William Ostler

Chapter 8

One day, Mother was puzzled to find me sitting in front of the TV with the sound turned off. Positioning herself in front of me so I could read her lips, she asked, "Justin, why did you turn off the sound? Couldn't you hear it?"

"I could hear it," I answered, "but I couldn't understand the words. It's like going to the zoo and trying to interpret monkey talk. It was too much chatter, and there's no point having the volume cranked up when I'm just reading lips."

There's a big difference between hearing and understanding. When I attended Father's concerts, I could hear the music, but I couldn't understand all the lyrics. But I loved hearing my father sing—and I still do, to this day.

My family spent a lot of time traveling with Father's concert tours. When we were out of school, we traveled on a big bus lined with bunk beds. We'd sleep on the bus and spend time with Father between concerts. His fans only saw the stage front end of show business. It's a lot different behind the scenes. Mother always hoped the theater would have a washer and dryer so she could take care of the laundry. If there was time to spare before the concert, Mother might find a zoo or some other attraction for us kids to visit. Of course we would always attend the performances.

Justin and Merrill on the tour bus

As always, when my family hit the road, my speech therapy became a family project. Maybe I would innocently point out the window at a beautiful old church with a steeple soaring to heaven and call, "Look at that shursh!"

Before I could even blink, someone would be sure to holler, "Justin said his c - h's wrong!" Then everyone would work with me and encourage me to give those consonants the explosive sound of "ch." By the time they were satisfied, the church I'd pointed out was in another state! I really appreciate my family loving me enough to play sound games over the endless miles so I could learn to speak. I credit every one of them in helping me to develop better speech.

Still, I have vivid memories of summer days when we weren't touring. My brothers and sisters finished practicing their instruments and were out playing while Mother and I stayed inside doing speech therapy. My eyes wandered to the window and the glorious wide-open spaces that seemed to call for me to come play. Other kids played on swings or ran laughing around the house. Sometimes it seemed that therapy went on and on with no rescue in sight. But I wasn't given a choice to give up or cut any corners off speech therapy time. Accepting that I had to do it was the only option I had. It was just part of my life.

My family's intervention helped me learn to survive in a chaotic world. I'm much better at one-on-one conversations, although I can't avoid group discussions all together. Since I often have a hard time plucking out words when there's a lot of background noise, I often lip read. If I can't follow what's going on, there's obviously a communication gap. It's been that way my whole life, and I've learned to accept it. I've also become a better listener by paying more attention to both audio and visual cues.

My lip reading skill has unexpected benefits. One time Travis and I went to a restaurant where a couple of guys wearing camouflage sat about thirty feet away from us. They looked like real outdoorsmen who had just returned from some kind of adventure. One of them gestured and spoke with great animation. The other leaned forward, arms folded on the table.

Being outdoorsmen ourselves, we were curious.

"Man," Travis said. "I sure wish I knew what they were talking about."

I focused my attention on the speakers for a few moments, then said, "His buddy harvested a big buck yesterday . . . twenty inches wide . . . up Hobble Creek."

Travis just stared at me, his eyes wide with amazement.

I shrugged. "You said you wanted to know."

I am able to lip read almost anything and anyone . . . except for Karl Malone of the Utah Jazz team of the NBA (National Basketball Association.) Every time he stood at the free throw line, I would watch his lips move as he handled the ball, but I couldn't decipher a single word. Was it another language or some private mantra that gave him super basketball skills? If anyone could come forward and tell me what he said, I'd be forever grateful. Unsatisfied curiosity can be a terrible thing.

With new technology available to us, I can hear a lot better than I used to, but I still miss out on conversations. Believe it or not, I've come to realize this is one of the greatest blessings I could ever receive. My hearing loss protects me somewhat from the incredibly noisy world we live in. As a result, I've had to put in more physical and mental exertion and listen more intently.

On another note, when I focus my listening skills on a spiritual level, I'm protected from distraction and other outside influences.

In this other quiet world that I can choose to live in, I've developed intensive focus that has helped me achieve more than anyone thought I could. My parents always knew I had it in me.

Just like I must rely on my hearing aids to help me physically hear, I must rely on my heart to spiritually hear and understand. When referring to my heart, I mean things spiritual, or what I like to call the Spirit of God. This is a concept that all individuals can participate in.

Helen Keller's statement, "The most beautiful thing in the world cannot be seen, heard, or touched. It can only be felt by the heart," is echoed in the Bible with our Lord and Savior's confirmation, "He that hath ears to hear, let him hear . . . ." He doesn't mean this in a physical sense, but rather a spiritual one. Or in other words, we need to listen and hear with our hearts.

It's easy to get caught up in a noisy world and forget to listen, so I find a quiet place. A quiet place for me can be anywhere and anytime because all I have to do is turn my hearing aids off. If you have no quiet place to turn to, use an ordinary place that grows quiet in the early morning before the world awakens or in the soft, sleepy night when everyone else has gone to bed. Get comfortable in this place, then let gentle waves of gratitude roll over you as you think about the small things you're grateful for. Let your heart grow warm and your breath slow as you expand your thoughts to the greater blessings in your life. Think about the things you like to do. Don't bring in feelings of frustration. Just experience the joy of feeling, as though all your dreams have come true and that the most wondrous blessings are making their way to you right now.

In the quiet stillness, be thankful.

Dream.

Be happy to simply breathe.

Be happy to be you.

Listen to your heart.

This is my place of solace; my quiet place; my sacred grove, where I often go. I call it "Utah's best hidden secret."

"For our light affliction, which is but for a moment, worketh for us a far more exceeding and eternal weight of glory."
— *II Corinthians 4:17*

Chapter 9

My father's whole life is music, so he expected that if his children were going to play instruments, they were going to play them well. That included me.

Some may ask how a deaf person could play music at all, let alone play it well. In my case, it may have started when people pointed out to my parents that my siblings could play music, but I couldn't. That was the wrong thing to say to my mother, because she takes challenges head-on.

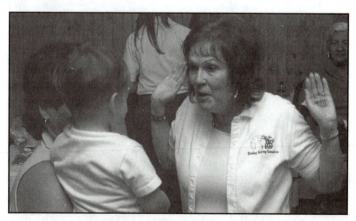

Mary Osmond entertaining a little boy
while on a Starkey Hearing mission.

Mother is a piano player who never took her music to a serious level. But she knew enough to help us play into our intermediate years. She taught us simple chords and scales and the main melody. When she couldn't keep up with us any more, she hired a piano teacher. Every morning she monitored my brothers and sisters at the piano while helping me with speech therapy. As soon as summer rolled around, Mother added piano lessons to my daily routine. Every time I tried playing the upper keys, I simply couldn't hear the high tones. At last, I learned to play by memorizing notes rather than listening to what I was playing. I never became really good at the piano.

A music teacher once told Mother that vibrations traveled through the entire violin when it was played. Sound vibrations are very important in deaf communication. They helped Uncle Virl and Uncle Tom learn how to tap dance. Once they got the sense of rhythm by feeling the floorboards vibrate under their feet, they would go into their routine of memorized steps. It may not have been perfect, but it was pretty amazing.

Justin learning to play the violin

Vibrations were also essential to the great composer Beethoven when he went deaf. He placed a metal stick against the piano and leaned it against his jaw to feel the vibrations in the instrument while it was being played. That is the same way I learned how to play the violin—and with a lot more success than the piano.

A lot of people have asked me, "With your hearing loss, how can you hear the notes?" The answer is that a violin is held against the chest by the pressure of the chin. Vibrations from the strings resonate through the jawbone and travel to the brain. It's a remarkable conduit for sound.

Mother started me at four years old with a 32nd size instrument. As I grew, she graduated me to a 16th size and then progressively larger ones. In spite of the fact that I could feel the vibrations while playing the strings, it took me a long time to learn how to play. There was frustration along the way. But my parents offered encouragement and motivation by telling me I could do it. At first my attention span could only handle ten minutes of practice here and ten minutes there, but I was proud to have music lessons like the other kids.

On the following page is a copy of my audiogram, which shows the decibel levels on the left side. The numbers running horizontally across the bottom are the frequencies. As the graph illustrates, the higher the pitch, the more decibels are needed for me to hear. Sound frequencies are lower on the extreme left and higher pitched as the numbers progress to the right. The Xs show the results of testing my left ear and the Os show the hearing level in my right ear.

With scant hearing in the high frequencies, I stayed away from high pitched notes as much as possible. Sometimes the high frequency notes were too difficult—if not impossible—for me to hear and play. My teacher suggested I move to a lower frequency instrument called a viola.

In spite of switching instruments, there were still times when I felt like I couldn't do it. This was a time when I simply wanted to give up. If I couldn't get the notes right, then what was the point? Yet I always found a way. I simply had to practice more. I decided that if I had to practice more hours to get it right, then so be it. Many times Mother would have to tell me to adjust my fingers on the strings because I couldn't hear that I was off-key. One note sounded pretty much like any other. I ended up having to memorize fingering positions. If the instrument wasn't in tune before I played, then my fingering got messed up.

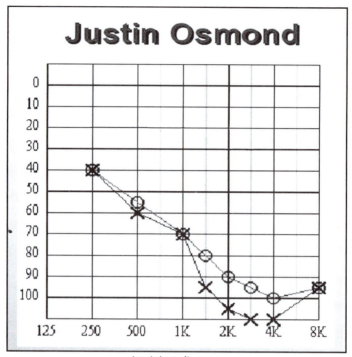

Justin's audiogram

At first, Father or my brothers would tune my instrument for me. Over time, Father helped me with intonation, and I learned to tune it myself. My brain heard the tuning over and over again until it memorized the sound. After it was implanted in my brain, I could do it.

Shane has perfect pitch, so Father would ask him to play a piece, then turn to me and say, "Justin, you play what Shane just played." I'd put that violin under my chin and play it. Father says I have perfect tonality, which is defined as organization of music around a single pitch.

Travis admits I'm a good drummer, which makes sense when you consider the vibrational nature of percussion. The thing that's funny is that after all the time we've spent together, Travis still hardly believes that I can play a violin. That's ironic coming from a guy who can play two recorders through his nostrils simultaneously and harmonize at the same time!

Father challenged his children to master each other's music while Mother urged us to play in different keys. "Play this in the key of 'C'," she'd say. Then, "Okay, now play it in the key of 'B flat.'"

Even though I was determined to learn music, it took me longer than the average hearing student. There were times I struggled so hard to play the violin that I hated practicing. Memorizing the notes and mastering the overall technique took me a very long time. Sometimes my brothers and I relieved the boredom by having sword fights with our bows. I can't tell you how many bows I've broken by using them as swords.

Of course my parents were very upset about that. An optimistic view of this situation is, "I'm deaf, so I don't have to hear my mother yelling at me!" In spite of the bow fights and everything else I put them through, I'm

Justin with his bow, which will inevitably turn into a sword

grateful that my parents never gave up on me. Ultimately I got pretty good on the viola and violin. Now I can play just as well as the next man.

Travis's first stringed instrument was a cello, but he hated it. He remembers practicing for what seemed like thirteen hours straight, trying to memorize a song. The only reason he did it was because he felt it was important to our parents. When he finally moved to a bass, he was much happier. I ended up playing the viola. Our brother Troy was on the cello while Shane joined our sisters Heather and Sheila on their violins. Sheila was so little when we first began performing that her biggest role was running out at the end of the concert and plucking a violin string. It brought a lot of laughs.

Since our string teacher was a tall man named Conrad Dunn, Father named our little music group "Big C and the Little Os."

Justin with Conrad Dunn

Father also came up with a fancy little move where Shane and I twirled our bows around in the air. Since we were standing on either side of Travis, when I lost control of my bow, it sailed through the air and clonked Travis on the head. That started another bow sword fight.

For a couple of years, we traveled all over the country performing at state and county fairs and school events. With a variety of singing, dancing, and instrumental numbers, we showed kids our age that they really could learn to play music.

One night, Father sat down with us at a family council and asked, "Do you want to be professional entertainers? If you do, I can help." We all looked at each other and read the same answer in everyone's eyes. None of us wanted to follow in Father's professional footsteps. He was hardly ever home, and we had enough of that lifestyle. Even though entertainment runs in our blood, my father also taught us to enjoy life's simple pleasures and not get caught up in the craziness life can offer. We chose to live a very simple lifestyle while still enjoying music. Doing two shows a day with Father when we lived in Branson, Missouri was as professional as we ever got.

While making music, professionals need to hear all the instruments in order to make the music ring out the way it should. Making subtle adjustments to their voices or instruments

Travis, Shane, and Justin as "Little Os"

is crucial to keeping in tune with the others.

The trouble for me was, whenever I played my viola in a group, all I could hear through my jawbone were the notes I played myself. From any musician's perspective, this is a real challenge. My whole life, I've never been able to hear the beautiful sound of blended chords and harmony, which is the very reason people enjoy concerts. I had to hope my instrument was in tune with everyone else's, work extra hard, and use more mental exertion to make sure I was on beat. I watched my stand partner's bow go up and down to check my rhythm. Because I couldn't completely hear everyone else in the orchestra or band, I figured I could at least play on the downbeat while hoping I was hitting the right notes.

My brothers probably don't know this, but I would always stand on the left of Shane. When I had a hard time with the tempo, I'd watch Shane's bow go up and down through the corner of my eye. Because I knew he was on beat, I would follow his rhythm. His bow was my metronome. If he wasn't on beat, then we were all in trouble.

Being onstage with my family became comfortable. We enjoyed being together, creating music, and making people happy. If the whole world was an onstage performance, then I would have been content.

But life had other lessons to teach me.

"We don't measure our success by the number of challenges we have, but by the number of challenges we overcome."

– Gordon B. Hinckley

Chapter 10

I started kindergarten at Manila Elementary School in Pleasant Grove, Utah. Not only was my early education a real struggle, but my social life wasn't so great, either. I had to wear a big FM hearing system consisting of a box that fastened to my belt. Wires snaked out of it to attach my jumbo hearing aids sitting behind my ears. I looked like a robot. If that wasn't bad enough, my teacher had to wear a large microphone box around her neck to amplify her voice into my hearing aids.

It's pretty normal for everyone to go through some kind of peer pressure, but imagine walking around wrapped up in wires. Being the only one looking like that was not a socially comfortable thing to do.

Mother did her best to help. Every year before school began, she would take me to meet the teachers and explain my situation. I knew she was there to look out for me and make sure I got proper treatment from the faculty and staff, but it was embarrassing at the time.

Each year my former speech therapist, Nancy Callaffee-Schenck, traveled from Colorado to meet with people involved in my education. She helped Mother choose the best schools for me and looked for very specific qualities in placement, such as who was willing to be flexible and communicate in a way I could comprehend. Nancy held in-service meetings with teachers who needed to know how to help me.

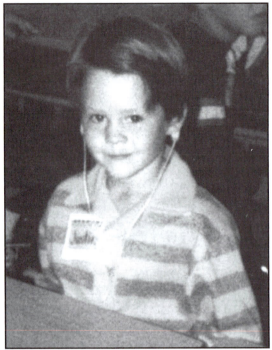

Justin wired for school

She and my mother also did school presentations so my classmates would know what hearing aids were and the best way to respond to me. She helped handle my schoolmate's fear and curiosity factors so they wouldn't treat me any differently.

I can still picture Mother standing up in front of the class asking, "Why do people wear braces? To straighten their teeth, of course. Why do some people use crutches or wheelchairs? To get places when they can't walk. Why do people wear glasses? You know it's because they can't see well without them. Justin wears his hearing aids because he can't hear well without them."

If the kids wanted to, Mother would let them try on my hearing aids and explain how they worked. "If they start squeaking, just poke Justin in the shoulder and tell him to push them in tight so they'll stop." Mother did everything she could to keep other children from making fun of me and my hearing aids.

Still, those first five years of elementary school kept Mother swimming, trying to keep me up to speed academically. In spite of the crash-training program, some teachers still weren't sure what to do with me. At that point in my education, I was still having speech therapy and learning how to talk. I had to simply survive the best I could.

One day I told Father I didn't want to go to school. When he asked me why, I told him that some kids made fun of my hearing aids. He looked at me and said, "So you've got hearing aids. Other people wear eyeglasses." He waited a moment, but when I didn't reply, he asked, "May I go to school with you?"

He walked me to my classroom. As soon as the teacher saw me, she announced in a loud voice, "Justin's here!"

Father approached her and quietly said, "Please don't do that. Don't make a big issue out of Justin arriving at school."

I appreciate my parents trying so hard, but in spite of anyone's best efforts there are always going to be bullies in the world. I got picked on and made fun of on a regular basis. I couldn't belong to certain groups because I didn't look the part or they didn't think I fit in.

One day after school, an older elementary school kid named Jared hooked his elbow around my neck, pretending to be my buddy. He led me around to the back of the school and beat me until I lay bleeding on the ground. He did this for no reason other than my hearing gear made me look out of the ordinary, and I talked differently than the other kids.

A girl from school saw Jared leave the scene. As soon as she saw me lying on the ground, she hurried to find Travis. By the time he reached the battleground, I was inside the building receiving first aid. Travis went looking for Jared instead. When he asked Jared if he had beaten me up, Jared admitted it, so Travis gave him a bloody nose.

His way of dealing with Jared may seem harsh, but Travis was my protector. He's always taken good care of me from the very beginning. To his credit, he never resented my parents' expectation that he would look after me. It was quite the opposite. He felt like he was born first in order to be my protector. He was always bigger and stronger than those who gave me a hard time, and he'd get upset with people who made me feel awkward about my speech. It's true that sometimes when he wanted my attention he thought he had to do something dramatic like hit me in the head with his shoe. I would return his message with one of my own. Although throwing things was one form of communication, we found more effective and less painful ways to get our point across. It was never awkward between us, not even when he was talking slowly to let me read his lips. It was as though we could hear each other with our hearts.

Travis was constantly observant to see if I could understand what someone was saying. He could tell by the look on my face if I was "getting it" or not. When Travis saw kids in school point to the big amplifier box around my neck and ask, "What's that gadget?" or "Why do you have to wear that?" or "Why do you talk funny?" or "Can you understand me?" Travis would run across the room to answer their questions for me. He was truly my brother's keeper.

Justin and Travis – "my brother's keeper"

My young mind could not understand why I was beaten up in the first place. I hadn't done anything to hurt anyone, so why did someone hurt me? It didn't just hurt my physical body. My self-esteem and confidence went down the drain, too. I was old enough to wonder why I was so different. I didn't want this, and it didn't seem fair. Why did I deserve to get punched for something over which I had no control? Why couldn't those kids who teased me realize how lucky they were? Why would God allow these undeserved trials to come upon me? Was I really so different from other people?

I quickly learned that these trials and experiences ultimately helped me develop a great deal of compassion for others. How can you be sympathetic toward someone else's pain if you've never been hurt yourself? It's strange to look back on my life and see how the most painful things turned out to be some of the best teaching experiences. I think it's safe to say that if I hadn't gone through that encounter and others like it, I would have less compassion, patience, and understanding in my adult life.

In today's society, people tend to judge the outward appearance. Consider the attractive popular kids in school. Everyone knows them, but they often have the fewest real friends. Popularity comes and goes, depending on the whims of people. You don't obtain friends by becoming popular, but by earning respect. Those who may be less popular can gain the respect of everyone around them. It's even possible to have respect from your enemies. At times, my elementary years seemed to be full of enemies.

"I am encouraged when after each struggle I gain a victory. I want to climb higher and higher until I finally reach the summit of my desire."

— Helen Keller

Chapter 11

I have a confession. As hard as I tried to learn what I was supposed to do in my first grade schoolwork, I sometimes copied other people's papers. I didn't do it because I was lazy, it was simply because I didn't understand what I was supposed to do. The teacher would explain the concept she was teaching, but since I couldn't hear very well, I couldn't always understand. More often than not I sat in class feeling very isolated because I was unable to comprehend the new material. When the teacher handed out worksheets, I sat and stared at mine, frustrated that I couldn't figure out what I was supposed to do. Even though I felt desperate, I was an independent little guy who didn't want to ask for help. None of the other kids seemed to have questions, and I wanted to be like them. I thought that raising my hand would draw unwanted attention to me. I figured that if I studied the paper long enough I might see some kind of pattern, and if I found one, I would memorize it and assume that's how every question on the paper worked. Unfortunately, that wasn't always the case.

Even though I felt bad about it, my frustration drove me to cheat by copying my neighbor's work. I didn't always do it, just a few times when I felt desperate. It all came to an abrupt end when I was finally caught. No matter what, if you cheat, you're going to get caught.

That's the hard way to learn. The good thing about it is that it also provided a valuable lesson for me in learning to ask for help.

Understandably concerned for my future, Mother and Father sat me down and told me that cheating is not right and was no way to get through life. Father said if I didn't understand, I shouldn't sit back and do nothing. He taught me to ask questions as many times as necessary in order to get the information I needed. He stressed that, even if someone laughed or I had to ask several times, it didn't matter. I was to get every question answered until I understood. After that heart-to-heart talk, I resolved that it was better to be embarrassed and ask for help, even if it meant raising my hand to say, "I don't get it," three or four times.

When Father visited my school after that talk, he stood at the back of the room and watched me raise my hand from the front row where I always sat. When the teacher acknowledged me, I'd say, "I'm sorry, can you repeat the question again?" Five minutes later, my hand was up again, and I'd say, "I'm sorry, but I didn't quite catch what you said. Do you mind saying it again?"

I'm sure that some teachers became frustrated with all my interruptions, but I quickly determined that I wasn't going to shy away from anything. I was going to learn what the answers were. That was the pivotal point when I really and truly understood that I had to work harder. It would require me to put forth more mental exertion, to really focus and listen, to meet with my teacher after school while other children were playing, and to take whatever time was necessary to work with my parents in order to understand the lessons. That was just the way it had to be for my life to head in the direction I wanted it to go.

Mother hired a babysitter for her younger children at home, then came to school to help me with class work I didn't understand. She would find out what I was going to learn the week before and go over it with me so that when the teacher taught it in class, I was familiar with it. Working harder to get through school made it so I didn't take anything for granted.

Most teachers quickly became accustomed to the microphone worn around their neck that amplified their voice into my hearing aids. But sometimes they'd get so comfortable with it that they'd forget to turn it off, and I would hear them in the bathroom or talking to other teachers in the faculty lounge.

One day I became the most popular kid in class. A couple of my classmates acted up, and the teacher took them out in the hall. She forgot to turn off her microphone, so I could hear everything she said. When the rest of the students realized that I had a pipeline to the hallway, they gathered around and asked me what she was saying and what was going to happen to their friends. I told them everything I could hear. They were impressed. From then on I gained a lot of respect from my classmates. They thought I had a pretty cool set-up.

Since I didn't do very well in group conversations, most teachers would stay after school and work with me one-on-one. I'm grateful to the teachers who went beyond normal expectations and played critical roles in helping me succeed.

After my family moved to Draper, Utah, I attended Waterford private school, which was voted as one of the best in the nation. Again, I was mainstreamed with hearing kids. I still had to work extra hard to keep up with my classmates. When a normal hearing student would read an assignment once, I had to read it two or three times. One of my challenges is problem solving, because logical reasoning stems from childhood brain development. When words and connections aren't formed at a young age, the brain can lag behind. I often felt like I was on the sidelines, missing out on all the action. Mother often saw me with a smile on my face while conversations buzzed all around me. It broke her heart because she realized I didn't understand what was being said.

One of the best moments of my mother's life took place when I was eight years old. We visited a fast food restaurant, and she watched me walk up to the counter and order my own hamburger. The cashier understood me well enough to complete the transaction. Mother sat down in the booth and cried. She was so happy to know I wouldn't starve because I could order a hamburger.

Mother was stunned at a parent-teacher conference where she was told, "Justin can't read." That was very hard for her to believe because she read to me all the time. When she did her own investigation, she was amazed to discover that, during school, I would read one line from left to right, then drop my gaze down to the next line and read it right to left. I seemed to have no understanding of the story I was reading. I simply read lines of words backward and forward as if they were rows of spelling words.

Strangely enough, when I read to my mother at home, I scanned each line from left to right, top to bottom, in traditional American fashion.

At the rate I was going, I'd never make it through high school, so Mother took action again. With Father's approval, she enrolled me in an after-school Sylvan Learning program, which fixed my reading problem. She also moved me from Waterford to another private school called Challenger, which proved to be a pivotal point in my education.

Justin in elementary school

"I am only one, but I am still one; I cannot do everything, but still I can do something; and because I cannot do everything, I will not refuse to do the something that I can do."

– Edward Hale

Chapter 12

One day I came home from school with a problem. I don't remember exactly what it was, but I remember being glad to see my father sitting in the family room with his back to me and a book in his hands. I called out, "Father? I need your help."

There was no response. With a little catch in my heart, I thought, *Maybe my father has developed a hearing loss.* I moved closer to him and said again, "Father? I need some help."

Again, no response.

I thought with alarm, *Oh, my goodness, my father must have a hearing loss. When did this happen?* I moved right behind him. "Father, can you hear me?"

Father turned his head and said, "Yes, Justin, for the third time, what do you want?"

Father had heard everything. It was clear that I was the one with the hearing loss. I couldn't change that part of my life by wishing. It really helped that my family accepted me and provided great examples of how to live.

If parents only knew what a critical role they play in their children's ability to learn, they would make good choices about spending time with their little ones. The enabling factor for a child's success is almost always a parent or relative. If a child has someone close to them in their early years who sets a good example, then that child has a solid foundation for a productive life. Father did me a great favor that day because he set an example regarding the importance of reading. Fathers are traditionally involved with their children's athletics, but children benefit immeasurably when fathers interact with them intellectually as well.

The truth is that even though reading is the most important social factor in American life today, a recent study showed that fathers read to children only 15% of the time, mothers 76% and others 9%. A Texas A&M study found that 40.2% of fathers never read to their children. [1] These statistics show that if a boy lives in a home where sports are emphasized all the time, the boy will typically show far less dedication to academics. He would typically spend less or even no time reading or doing schoolwork. The end result is higher athletic scores, but lower school grades.

If children reach middle school without encountering a reading male role model, the idea that reading is for girls will already be lodged in their minds. We must short-circuit this trend by showing boys that a father can do both. Dad can play basketball, then read the paper Saturday morning. He can play catch with his children in the afternoon and read in the evening. In the home, only 57% of children aged three through five are read to every day by a family member. [2] Children who are read to at least three times a week by a family member are almost twice as likely to score in the top 25% on tests. [3]

My parents taught me the importance of education. I knew from the first time I kicked a soccer ball that if I wanted to play college sports some day, I'd still need to have passing grades. The simple rule was that if you didn't keep your academics up, you weren't on the team. If you're all sports and no education, there's no balance, so when the time comes to provide for a family, you're in trouble. Paternal involvement also has positive psychological effects, including less depression, higher self-esteem, and fewer behavior problems. [4]

The Commission on Reading, organized by the National Academy of Education and the National Institute of Education, issued a 1985 report titled, *Becoming a Nation of Readers*. Among its primary findings was that the single most important activity toward success was reading aloud to children both at home and in school. Reading aloud was more important than worksheets, homework, assessments, book reports, and flashcards. One of the cheapest, simplest, and oldest tools of teaching proved to be a better teaching tool than anything else available.

So how does a person tap into this powerful means of success that doesn't even require a high school diploma? Put simply, the more you read, the better you get at it; the better you get at it, the more you like it; and the more you like it, the more you do it. The more you read, the more you know, and the more you know, the smarter you grow. [5]

According to the 2004 National Assessment of Educational Progress, "Reading is more important than ever in an increasingly complicated, information-rich world. Basic literacy no longer suffices. In higher education and the workplace, young people must handle an array of complex texts—narratives, repair manuals, scholarly journals, maps, graphics, and more. Unfortunately, more than 8 million U.S. students in grades 4-12 struggle to read, write, and comprehend adequately. Only three out of ten eighth graders read at or above grade level." [6]

The National Center for Education Statistics reports that readers who fall significantly behind risk school and workplace failure. In 2003, only three-fourths of high school students graduated in four years. [7]

Charles Murray said, in The Chronicle Review, "It has been empirically demonstrated that doing well (B average or better) in a traditional college major in the arts and sciences requires levels of linguistic and logical/mathematical ability that only 10-15% of the nation's youth possess." [8]

Reading gave me better communication skills and opened doors that emphasized the same vocabulary that I had trouble hearing. Reading made me normal. I could have just as great adventures in the pages of books as the next boy. It also helped level the educational playing field. If I couldn't hear it, at least I could read it. Reading is the one tool that reaches across all fields of study. Not only do English teachers read, but historians, shop teachers, stage crew, and even math teachers. How else would you solve all those story problems?

A National Endowment for the Arts survey showed that adult reading was down 22%, with only 46.7% of 17,000 adults surveyed reading any fiction. When the survey expanded to include newspapers or any kind of book or magazine, the figure rose to only 50% of adults. In short, half of America is illiterate. [9]

An inexpensive fifteen minutes of reading to a child each day is the most valuable, yet most underused, educational tool available to everyone. Maybe it's underused because it is so simple. I cannot stress enough the change it made in my life for my parents to model reading. If it weren't for my literacy skills, I wouldn't be able to write this book. Even if you're not a good reader now, you can keep practicing. It doesn't matter how old you are. Get busy and find books that are of interest to you. Even if you read only one page a day, you'll make a definite difference, not only in your own life, but in the life of a child. And that can make all the difference in the world.

"It's better to appreciate the things we don't have than to have things and not appreciate them."

– *Ezra Taft Benson*

Chapter 13

Travis thinks I'm sometimes too innocent and trusting. Perhaps Travis is too rigid at times. In spite of the fact that we tend to take opposite views of things and tackle problems differently, we get along great. It's pretty much the same with the rest of my family. We've never gotten into any real big fights. I don't know why, unless it was because our father was gone so much, and we felt the need to band together. When Father was gone, Travis filled in as the man of the house and generated a feeling of respect among us all.

That's not to say that everything was perfect. We had our moments, as typical siblings do—especially the brothers. Sometimes we got into arguments. More than once when I didn't want to hear what anyone was saying, I'd turn off my hearing aids. It was like, "Hey, this conversation's over." *Flip,* and I'd turn them off.

Turning off my hearing aids came in handy for sleeping, too. One night, twelve-year-old Travis was babysitting for the first time. We were in our parents' room with the TV on, and eighteen-month-old Troy was asleep in the crib. Mother and Father had taken infant Sheila and gone out for ice cream. I had my hearing aids out, and at some point I fell asleep.

Suddenly, Travis was startled by the home security motion detector's silent alarm. Heart pounding, he quickly checked the security system's wall monitor. Once, when the security system activated, we called the police before discovering that our dogs had triggered the alarm.

That wasn't the case this time. Travis saw the frightening image of two strange men easing their way through our front door. Hair rose on the back of his neck as the intruder's dark clothing melted into ominous shadow along the dark hallway they crept along. Heart in his throat, Travis made a desperate decision. Popping open the bedroom door, he dashed to the next bedroom, bursting in to collect our little brother and sister. His grab for Heather's sleeping form caught her hair. At the same time, he snagged a slumbering Shane's arm. Ignoring their sudden cries, he got a better hold on Heather and dragged them both into the dubious safety of our parents' room. Slamming the door, he locked it and took in a long, shuddering breath. In the time it had taken him to collect the rest of his family, the intruders had made their way down the hall, past the kitchen, and into the family room. The sound of the slamming door reverberated through the house, but it didn't seem to faze the prowlers. That worried Travis even more. With shaking fingers, he dialed the bedroom phone and got Mother on the line. He told her the situation the best he could with his voice raised over the wails of Heather, Shane, and the newly awakened Troy.

"Hang on, Travis," Mother said, forcing her voice to stay calm. "Father's on another phone with the police. They're on their way. You just stay put, do you hear me?"

"Yes," Travis whispered into the receiver, even though it was no secret to anyone on either side of the bedroom door where we were hiding. Travis watched in breathless terror as the prowlers moved toward the double doors of the master bedroom. They may or may not have known that their movements were being tracked on the monitor. They didn't seem to care because they kept on coming until there was only an inch of wood standing between us and them.

Passivity is not one of Travis's strengths. He decided to act. With a curious mix of panic and bravado, he dropped the phone, grabbed Father's shotgun, and aimed the barrel at the door. Raising his voice above the children's screams, he yelled, "I'm going to shoot!"

Travis heard Mother shout something through the phone, but her faint words were lost in the cries of her younger children. Travis didn't want to ignore her, but he was too busy to pick up the phone. He gripped the stock tighter and slid his finger over the trigger. Eyes glued to the monitor, he watched the intruders glance at each other. One of them shoved his thumb back over his shoulder, then they both turned and headed back the way they'd come.

He'd done it! Travis stood taller and moved his finger to the trigger guard. There was no doubt that he'd defended his home and family. He was a man now. Feeling like a hero, Travis strode over to the double doors and recklessly let himself out. Creeping along the wall with the gun barrel staring down the hallway ahead of him, he slowly pursued the retreating enemy. He came in sight of the front door just in time to watch the two men sneak outside. With a curious mixture of relief and jubilation, he made his way back to the bedroom and did his best to calm Heather, Shane, and Troy.

I slept through the whole thing.

The next morning, feeling invigorated after a good night's rest, I got to the breakfast table and looked around in surprise. Everyone else had bloodshot eyes and looked like they'd been through a hurricane. "What's wrong?" I asked.

Everyone stared at me for a moment before bursting into a volley of explanations that were too jumbled to make sense. Finally, they slowed down and spoke one at a time so I could get a clear understanding of the previous night's drama. Some of them were rather upset with me for sleeping through the ordeal. On some level, they wished they had the ability to turn off their hearing so they could sleep well, but my family didn't hold it against me for long. They are truly my best friends, and they've always accepted me as though I am no different from them in any way. That has been a huge impact for good in my life. Psychologically, it was a key factor in my success, because they made me feel like I was just a normal person who could do as well as anyone else.

I will admit that I enjoy sleeping soundly. It's so quiet when I take my hearing aids out, and I don't have to hear the cows mooing or the rooster's cockadoodledoo. But what would have happened that fateful night if I'd been alone? Obviously, my inability to hear can put me in danger. It's just another aspect of my life that hearing people don't generally consider. We need to be grateful for every gift we have, no matter how small. If we walk with a limp, at least we can walk. If we don't learn things as fast as others, at least we can learn. If we have 10% hearing, at least we can hear something.

Justin, Travis, and Shane
Brothers watch each other's backs

If we have all of our hearing, we should not take it for granted, nor should we take people with hearing loss for granted. The fact is, the more you learn about a different way of life, the better your understanding becomes.

I believe that Lowell L. Bennion makes a good point in his quote, "An essential ingredient of integrity, often overlooked, is self-acceptance. We cannot be strong integrated personalities unless we learn to rejoice in our own individuality, in being who we are. Self-rejection divides and confuses the self. To have integrity we must come to terms with ourselves as persons. By this self-approval I do not mean self-satisfaction, but only the confidence of being who we are, so we can function freely and fully as integrated human beings. Integrity gives us a sense of wholeness, unity, strength, security, and peace of mind. If we have integrity, we fight ourselves least and therefore have more strength for the outside battle. Integrity is the first law of life. We cannot give ourself to others until we have secured it within and for ourselves."

"Be patient, be righteous, keep an eternal perspective, and you will be protected."

– Russell M. Nelson

Chapter 14

My teacher at Challenger School was no stranger to me. Jackie Casdorph had been to my house the summer before my sixth grade year to help me study. Even after the school year began, she made periodic visits to my home to give me additional academic assistance.

The students at Challenger gave me a few curious looks when I showed up wearing my robot hearing aids, but once they realized I wasn't a bizarre science experiment or someone's show-and-tell, they accepted me—hearing aids and all. Their nonchalant attitude gave me the courage I needed to put myself out and participate in activities.

Ms. Casdorph was very considerate. She made sure to face me whenever she spoke so we communicated well.

Under her tutelage we played a multiplication game called, "Around The World." I have an affinity for math, which probably comes from not having to speak much in order to do it. It was a great day when I discovered that I was the only student who beat Ms. Casdorph at straight multiplication. It was a very narrow margin, and it only happened once, but for a time I was the multiplication world champion. That was a great boost to my confidence.

On the other end of the education scale from math is reading. For someone like me, reciting memorized pieces in front of the whole class

Justin wearing body aids to help him hear

is worse than reading. At this point in my life, I was still learning how to speak, so I fretted and worried over the required classroom speech.

When it was my turn, I made my way slowly to the front of the room, a feeling of certain dread blanketing my heart. I avoided eye contact, afraid I would read contempt, derision, and an intent to get me after school in the other students' eyes. I stumbled through my first piece—which was mercifully short—then fled to my desk and collapsed onto my seat.

Nothing bad happened.

The next time I had to recite, I risked a glance up at the faces before me. No one crossed their eyes or shook their fist. After a few turns speaking in front of the class, I realized I could do it without fearing any dire consequences. That made me feel pretty good. No one made fun of me or hurt me in any way. This opened up whole new possibilities. Completing that difficult requirement gave me the confidence to believe that I could do an adequate job of public speaking.

At that stage in life, I was a really good lip reader. My classmates and I played a game where they would stand as far from me as they could across the playground and mouth words. Then I would interpret what they said. I could always tell.

The playground was a noisy, confusing place that didn't let me hear what went on around me, yet I loved getting down and dirty in a rowdy game of soccer. I had the uncanny ability to sense where people were on the field. It was the strangest thing. I can't explain it, but I'm grateful for it, because it let me be a team player.

As my confidence grew, so did my bravado. That spring, Ms. Casdorph was in charge of the school program. This not only included speaking parts, but singing and dancing as well. When I saw the signup sheet, I had a sudden urge to break out of my cocoon. Before carefully thinking it through, I signed up. When my name came up, I walked into the sound room to audition for a vocal solo. If she was surprised to see me, she didn't show it.

"Hello, Justin," she greeted me with a warm smile. "Are you ready to audition?"

I nodded and stepped up to the microphone. Pulling it into a position close to my mouth, I gripped the stand just below the mike and sang for all I was worth. It felt good, except for one thing. When I finished, I turned to my teacher. "Ms. Casdorph, I'm afraid your microphone is out of tune."

How could she keep a straight face? But she did. She thanked me for bringing it to her attention and said I could go.

Of course, now I know I was the one out of tune. You might think that after pointing out my own limitations, a casting director would refuse to let a boy who was deaf sing in the show. A normal-hearted director would have given me a silent part. But Ms. Casdorph did not have a normal heart. Hers was extraordinary. Maybe she gave me a solo because she recognized my wanting it so bad that I put myself up for possible ridicule. Maybe it was because she had a leftover solo. Maybe it was because I was the son of the lead singer of the Osmonds. Maybe it's because she knew it would mean the world to me.

For whatever reason, Ms. Casdorph believed that I could do extraordinary things, and she helped me believe it, too. She gave me a solo, exemplifying her personal philosophy of sixth grade as the time when kids who feel confident and good about themselves can move on to junior high school and continue making good decisions. On the other hand, a sixth grader who doesn't feel like a good person may face a few rough years until they figure out that they are intrinsically good.

I was so proud to stand up and sing for the audience and for my family. Father sat beside Mother, watching and listening with a smile on his face. Then he ducked his head, pulled out a tissue, and wiped his eyes. I was so touched that he would cry for joy over me, his son, just for singing a solo in a school play. That experience gave me enough confidence that by the end of the year, I felt like I could do anything I put my mind to.

Then the school administration took me by surprise. They suggested that I take sixth grade over again. I talked it over with my parents, who asked how I would like having Ms. Casdorph again. I couldn't argue with that, so my parents agreed with the administrators' assessment. The second time through sixth grade didn't give me as much time to work with Ms. Casdorph, however. Other teachers spent more time with me, some even allowing me to take home educational videos so I could watch them as many times as I wanted. I tried putting subtitles on them, which didn't always work.

I finally acknowledged that I could do just as well as my classmates if I didn't try to imitate them. I had to realize that I could never enjoy the convenience of having an I-pod playing in one ear while listening to the teacher with the other. I could not concentrate on my paper to take notes because I had to put my full attention toward lip-reading. Have you ever tried keeping your eyes on someone while writing what they say at the same time? You should try it just for fun. This is the way I had to do it, whether I wanted to or not. If I glanced down, I might miss something important. It was just another example of having to put more mental and physical exertion into learning compared to my peers.

After repeating sixth grade, I got another surprise. Testing so far ahead of the other graduating sixth graders made it so I completely leapfrogged over seventh grade. It was exciting for me to be back in my regular eigth grade class at Crescent View Middle School. My first day there, I checked my schedule to see I had a teacher named Mrs. Miller. There was nothing remarkable about her name, but when I found her classroom, I stopped and stared in amazement. I'd found a miniature Disneyland, minus the rides. The clock on the wall showed Mickey Mouse's arms keeping perfect time, there was a Donald Duck pencil sharpener, and other Disney characters everywhere; on wall posters, decorating the chalkboard, sitting among the shelves of books, and scattered across Mrs. Miller's desk. With such a playful outlook on life, Mrs. Miller, more commonly known as "The Disney Woman," became a magical oasis of fun and learning for me.

The music department held another wonderful surprise in the form of Lois Swint, a violinist for the Utah Symphony. She certainly had incredible violin skills, and she made sure I learned to improve my skills, too. I also appreciated Marian Wright's patience and talent in teaching me viola. There were many wonderful doors that opened for me at Crescent View. I was privileged to earn several academic honors, including our Viking mascot's "Viking of the Month" award. What's more humbling is that I was fortunate enough to receive the award multiple times in one year from the faculty. They voted for students who met citizenship, punctuality, letter grade, and attendance requirements.

Being close to my peers and making great academic strides made me feel pretty good about myself and my chance for success in life. This created such hope that I want to share the message with the world that hope is so much better than hopelessness. I can't stress enough how even just a little bit of kindness goes a long, long way.

"Physical strength is measured by what one can carry. Spiritual strength is measured by what one can bear."

— Spencer W. Kimball

Chapter 15

I was planning on attending Alta High School. While I was still in middle school, the high school soccer coach came to Crescent View and asked me to be on his team. My parents changed my class schedule so I could play. I felt right at home with the big boys and Coach Mitchell. That year, we won the State Championship. I also competed as part of the AAA soccer team "Sparta" in matches all over the United States. We ultimately won the national eigth place rank at a tournament in Atlanta, Georgia.

I always played my best, but one critical moment came when I wanted to show my father what I was capable of. Let me say first that my father has always been by my side—if not physically, then I knew he was thinking of and praying for me. He's always inspired me to greatness, telling me to be the best I can be.

This incident happened on one of the rare days Father could attend my soccer game. I was no different than every other son who wanted to make his father proud. I took my main starter position of mid-center halfback, ready to show Father what kind of soccer player I had become.

For some reason, I wasn't playing up to my full potential. To my great disappointment, Coach took me off the field. It seemed I couldn't do anything right, so I stood on the sidelines, huffing and puffing and feeling like a failure. I was so down-hearted and churning with angry, fearful emotions that I didn't notice Father leave the stands. When I finally noticed him walking toward me, I thought, *Great. How can I possibly explain my poor performance?* Then I quickly set my face in a mask of pretended indifference.

When Father walked up beside me, the first thing he did was put his arm around me and say, "Son, I'm so proud of you. I know you're doing the best you can, and that makes me proud."

The ice around my heart melted. I began telling him how sorry I was that I wasn't playing my best. I tried to tell him I didn't know why I wasn't doing anything right and that I felt like such a failure.

What Father said next proved that while Mother taught me to listen with my ears and brain, my father taught me to listen with my heart. "Son," he said, "if you fear failure, then you don't have the faith sufficient enough to believe that God will lead you to your final destiny."

His words engraved themselves in my heart and put a stop to my self-pity. I felt instantly empowered. The understanding in my mind was so clear that as soon as you fear anything, you lose the ability to do the very thing you're capable of doing. That day, Father made me realize that I could be a winner no matter what the score. I shouldn't go out on the field in fear of doing things wrong. Instead, with a heart full of faith, I should simply go out there and play the game to the best of my ability for the sake of enjoying the experience.

After that talk I went out on the field and scored a goal for my father. Then we went out and celebrated with the biggest milkshakes ever. But guess what? My father would have bought that milkshake for me even if I hadn't scored a goal.

At another game Father attended, we were paired against a California team where every player looked twice my size. I was playing forward position, and I'll admit that I was a little intimidated. "Father," I said, "I just don't know if I'm able to do this."

Father looked me in the eye and said, "Son, you're going to run like a deer." With this encouragement, I went out and played hard. But so did the other team. In the midst of the action, someone smashed me in the head hard enough that pain exploded out my ears. If I was a deer, I'd taken a bullet. Dazed, I staggered toward the sidelines while trying to see through tears of pain and frustration. When I reached my

Merrill with Justin on the soccer field sidelines

hands up to cover my aching ears, my right hand touched something warm and wet. Startled, I yanked it away, horrified to see bright red blood smeared against my palm.

My eyes darted to the crowd where I found my father, his face full of concern. I headed straight for him. We discovered that one of my hearing aids had broken and cut my ear. Once the wound was treated, Father said, "Now this is a blessing."

I stared at him in frank disbelief. Had I lip read him right?

Father put his hands on my shoulders and looked me in the eyes. "You don't need those hearing aids to play," he said. "They're a distraction. You never hear the coach anyway. Just focus on the ball and whoever's coming after you. Now go out there and kick that ball!" Once I was back in the game, I followed his advice and managed to score a couple of goals. We ended up winning the game.

Sometimes my battles were not against other teams but against my limitation of having to wear hearing aids. By this time, I'd gone through many different brands of hearing products. Every time I got new ones, it was like breaking in a new pair of shoes. Not only did it take time to get used to wearing them, but I had to determine how much sweat they could take. Unlike most people, I happen to sweat like Niagara Falls. This is not good for electronics, and the old style behind the ear hearing aids were particularly susceptible to rivers of sweat. Throughout the game, I'd battle mental anxiety, thinking, *I hope my hearing aids stay alive.* When I was worried they might short out, I'd run to the sidelines, unhook them from my ears and hand them to my mother for safekeeping. Sometimes I played so hard I wouldn't get them off in time, and everything would suddenly go quiet. Yet in that quiet time, there was complete focus on the game. I couldn't always hear my teammate call, "I'm open." Yet I still had a sense of player position on the field.

Even when my hearing aids were working, I couldn't hear the coach half the time. Sometimes after the game, my mother would say, "Justin, did you hear them scream after you made that third goal?"

I'd say, "No. Did they really?"

Mother had me wear a sweatband to try to keep my hearing aids dry. It worked marginally well, but it wasn't foolproof. I went through a lot of challenges like that, but everyone has challenges. Thinking life has cheated you out of something you thought you deserved doesn't excuse you from living up to your full potential. Every single one of us gets our own share of heavy stones, whether they're disappointment, sorrow, or anything else that might weigh us down. But what do we do with them? Do we build a bridge or a wall?

Think about your deepest desire. Now think about what you are willing to do about it. You need to know your levels of desire and willingness in order to overcome trials. Perseverance, patience, and physical and mental exertion are critical keys to removing obstacles that stand in the way of your progression.

So it's up to you to decide. Do you want your goal bad enough to keep going when all else fails?

"Faith precedes the miracle."

– Spencer W. Kimball

Chapter 16

One summer I went with my family on vacation to Lake Powell. It's a great recreation spot. I fully intended to fill the week with fun and adventure, which included riding jet skis—the closest thing I know to riding a four wheeler on water.

As mentioned earlier, hearing aids and water don't mix. Not only are the batteries at risk of shorting out, but the electronic components of the hearing aid itself are not waterproof. So before riding the jet ski that first day, I took out my hearing aids, carefully slid them into a black vinyl carrying pouch, and secured the Velcro fastener. Then I set the pouch inside a mini glove compartment on the jet ski and slammed the door shut. I was ready to take off for the ride of my life over miles of water before heading back toward camp.

I had a great time riding through narrow canyons and across broad expanses of sapphire blue water. When the sun sank low in the sky, I started back for camp in high spirits. It was only when I glanced down at the open glove compartment that horror shot through me. How long had that little door been open? I bent down to search inside for my hearing aid pouch, but it was gone. My heart plummeted, and the joy of the day drained away. I didn't care about the sunny skies, sparkling water, or magnificent cliffs on all sides. My hearing aids were gone. How could I ever hope to find them when they were lost somewhere in miles and miles and miles of deep water? There was no way I could know when the compartment flew open. There was no way I could predict where the hearing aids could be in all that vast wetness. Besides, they were in a pouch that was not water proof, so what good would they be even if I did find them? By then I had a really great relationship with my hearing aids. They were like the air I needed to breathe. I was so heartbroken, it was worse than when my dog died. I didn't see how I could live without them. I was so depressed because I still had a week of Lake Powell vacation ahead of me. With no hearing aids, I wouldn't be able to enjoy conversations around the campfire with my family. I would miss out on so much.

After allowing enough time to feel sorry for myself, I decided to ride back over the water and find my hearing aids. Anybody in their right mind would think that was the craziest idea ever—especially if they knew how huge Lake Powell reservoir is. But I've been known to do crazy things, like playing a violin well enough to perform when I can't even hear. I believe in miracles.

One morning when I was sixteen, I awoke and put my hearing aid in my right ear. I couldn't hear a thing. Frightened, I checked the battery, but it was fine. In near panic, I put in my left hearing aid. I still confronted a wall of silence. I'd suddenly lost all my hearing, and it scared me nearly to death. No one knows exactly why it happened. I'd suffered some fluid buildup inside my ear that was causing migraines. I also had a dietary restriction against salt because too much could negatively affect my hearing. Either of these issues could have been the cause, or it could have stemmed from an unknown condition.

My family fasted and prayed for me, along with many friends. My father gave me a blessing. Nothing happened for three days. I suffered in complete silence, which was frightening in its tenacity. I tried to imagine going through life with no hearing at all. I cried and prayed and hoped, between bouts of despair. On the third day, I woke up to discover with great joy that my hearing had been fully restored. There was no medical explanation, so I said a heartfelt prayer of gratitude and called it a miracle. At times like that, I'm grateful to have a father who is worthy to give me a blessing when called upon.

Now I was ready for another miracle.

If you've never ridden a jet ski, you may not know that it leaves a faint trail of tiny white bubbles in the water. Knowing that I had a one in a million chance of finding my hearing aids, I said a prayer as I turned around and began following the faint trail I'd made minutes earlier. Keeping my eyes open, I scanned the water, searching for any sign of the missing pouch. As I rode along, the white trail grew fainter and fainter. Soon there would be nothing left. I gritted my teeth and kept going. The prayer, "Please help me find my hearing aids, please help me find my hearing aids," ascended to Heaven with each breath I took.

The nearly transparent trail curved slightly to the right. I followed it, continually scanning the water, when suddenly the lowering sun struck something small, square, and shiny floating on the water. I slowed down while my heart sped up. I stopped and bent closer to see what it was. My soul leaped with joy when I recognized my hearing aid pouch. I bent down and scooped it out of the lake with shaking fingers. I carefully opened it. To my great relief, both hearing aids were still there. It was no great surprise, but I was disappointed to see that they were wet. I immediately took out the batteries and dried the hearing aids as best I could. Then I rode back to camp, parked the jet ski, and set about carefully drying every single dial and electrode of those hearing aids. I used a blow dryer on a low setting to make sure they were as dry as they could get. When I had done the best I could, I waited for an hour, praying with my whole heart and soul that they would come to life—even if it was only long enough for me to hear for the rest of the week.

An hour went by. I took a deep breath and pulled out the fresh set of batteries that I always carried with me. I placed them in the hearing aids and, with a final prayer, slid them into my ears. They worked great!

What are the odds of finding a tiny black vinyl pouch floating in miles and miles of water—a task worse than finding a needle in a haystack? What are the odds of bringing completely submerged electronics back to life?

It was another miracle.

"Be believing, be happy, don't get discouraged, things will work out."

— *Gordon B. Hinckley*

Chapter 17

My father's show was rated the best entertainment in Branson, Missouri. My father always magnified his role as husband, father, and grandpa, and I've always been grateful for that. Unfortunately, his job required him to be gone a lot. As a result, Mother decided we should all move to Missouri in order to spend more time with him.

This is ironic, considering that she never showed up for their first date. At the time she agreed to the blind date, Mother couldn't name even one Osmond song. Second thoughts crept in. How could she stand an evening with an egotistical Osmond whose face was recognized all over the world? She was a simple Utah farm girl who had no tolerance for pomposity, so she simply didn't show up.

That could have been the end of it. Who would blame Father for crossing her off his list? He had plenty of other options for dating. Yet in spite of Mother's snub, he gave her one more chance. She showed up the second time, was able to get past the Osmond image, and fell in love with Merrill. I'm so grateful to this day for my parents. They are truly the best parents any kid could ask for.

Moving to Missouri was a big change for all of us, but it was the worst for Travis. He was on the Alta High School football team, had a great girlfriend, and simply didn't want to go. In his unhappiness, he looked at me and demanded, "Why aren't you upset about moving?

The walls could be falling down around you, and you wouldn't care!"

I think I would. I'd stand in a doorway or something.

In spite of Travis's protests, we packed up and moved halfway across the country. Mother was determined that our new home would not detract from our enunciation. After crossing the Missouri border, she turned to us and warned, "The first one of you who says 'ya'all,' I'm going to kick in the butt." It's funny that she was the first one.

Now the pattern of my school years repeated, with each successive year of high school spent in a different building with unfamiliar students and a new mascot. Attending a new school every year has its pros and cons. I met a lot more people, but felt like a freshman all over again. That in itself would be a challenge for anyone. But showing up in my gigantic hearing aids with no one knowing my background made it even more challenging. The students didn't know how to respond to me. It was like I was reinventing the wheel every time I went to a new school.

In Branson, Missouri, the Osmonds already had a reputation. The kids in school didn't really know my siblings or me. They only knew that my father was an entertainer. We were just down-to-earth kids who wanted to make friends. But out of jealousy or whatever motivation makes bullies tick, many students had the assumption that we thought we were "all that" because our father was famous. They would either pointedly ignore us or sneer at us and call us names. On top of that, I was targeted for ridicule because I had a hearing loss. Eventually, I managed to cultivate a few dear friends. Some of them actually took carbon-copy notes during class that helped me in my studies.

One thing about Branson High School that made it especially foreign was that it had no soccer program. Knowing how much it meant to me, Mother helped me find the closest community soccer team, which happened to be a two hour drive to Joplin, Missouri. So Mother hauled everyone there for my games and tournaments. Every game or performance we Osmonds had was a family affair. My sisters Heather and Sheila would stand on the soccer field sidelines and make up all sorts of cheers for me. It was fun to have my own personal cheerleaders.

Our family support extended to joining Father onstage, where we performed in front of 2,400 people daily. We danced, sang, and played our instruments. It was especially rewarding when I played the violin, because a lot of people said I would never be able to do it.

The only downside of our performances was they generated more unwanted attention from our classmates. They not only made fun of our musical abilities, but jeered at our religion. Strangely enough, until 1976, it was technically legal to exterminate a Mormon in Missouri due to the infamous Governor Boggs' exterminating order issued October 27, 1838. Missouri Governor Christopher S. Bond took that law off the books shortly before we moved there. Despite the challenges and turmoil we faced, I'm humbled to say that I'm a member of The Church of JESUS CHRIST of Latter-day Saints. I have no intention of forcing my religion on anyone. I respect others' beliefs and know that God is no respecter of persons. One of our fundamental beliefs is that all people may worship however they wish.

It's sad when people go out of their way to be cruel, especially if they profess belief in the teachings of any spiritual leader who encourages loving others as themselves. One day my little brother refused to get on the bus to go to school.

Mother bent down to 9-year-old Troy and asked, "What's wrong?"

Troy was reluctant to answer, but Mother persisted. Finally, Troy looked up with tears in his eyes and blurted, "If I tell, he'll kill me."

Shocked, Mother led Troy to the couch, sat down, and pulled him onto her lap. With gentle coaxing, she finally got him to tearfully admit that there was a boy at school who followed him around with a knife, threatening him at every opportunity.

Mother immediately called the school and told the principal what Troy had said. That day, the principal watched closely and saw a boy follow Troy around while brandishing a knife. Although the principal took the knife away and had a talk with the fourth grader, the principal didn't seem to think it was a very big deal. After all, they were just kids, and it was only a pocketknife. He dismissed it almost as casually as if they'd been playing cowboys and Indians.

We actually had teachers flunk us purely out of spite and not because we'd earned a failing grade. Students would move out of the center of the hallway and press their backs against the walls when they saw us coming. We were spit on, drugs were planted in our lockers, and our car tires were slashed in the school parking lot.

Former Miss America Heather Whitestone McCallum with Justin

Actress Marlee Matlin with Justin

It's sad when anyone is treated unfairly. Why can't people learn to read the inner pages of the book before judging the outside cover and casting it away? If our co-students had bothered to get to know us better, then a lot of problems could have been avoided.

I have several friends with hearing impairments who faced their challenges head-on with incredible results. Heather Whitestone became Miss America. Marlee Matlin became an Academy Award winning actress.

Lou Ferrigno became a world champion bodybuilder, which led to his acting breakthrough as television's Incredible Hulk.

Not everyone knows that Lou took up bodybuilding because he was the target of relentless childhood torment over his severe hearing impairment. Developing huge muscles was his way of payback. He hit the gym until he got big enough to beat anyone who might dare give him a hard time about being deaf.

I don't care who you are, being able to defend yourself is an appealing skill. When the Hulk invited me to work out at the gym with him, I was ecstatic. I used slightly smaller weights than he did, but I saved face by doing more than one rep.

If only I'd had bigger muscles when a couple of bullies cornered me in the Branson High School hallway. Those big football players shoved me up against a locker with startling force. I was terrified. I hadn't done anything to them. I didn't remember ever speaking to them. With my

Justin with Lou Ferrigno, "The Incredible Hulk"

toes barely touching the ground, one of them scowled and said, "Hey, stupid, you shouldn't be here." At that moment, while my body shook with fear, I honestly wished I wasn't there.

"Yeah," his friend growled, giving me a shake hard enough to rattle my teeth. "You are a total freak. Hey, weirdo, lemme see your hardware." He made a grab for one of my hearing aids, but I twisted my head in time to turn it away. He grabbed my hair and yanked. "Listen to me when I'm talking to you, punk!" Then he sneered. "Oh, yeah, that's right, you can't!"

The other laughed. "He's too stupid to know what we're saying!"

Of course I wasn't too stupid to know what they were saying or to miss the foul language they used to emphasize their malicious remarks. I was really scared. What was I supposed to do? What could I do? They were nearly twice as big as me, and there were two of them.

Then they started shoving me around, which was really frightening because every time I get hit in the head there's a chance I can lose more hearing. I have precious little as it is, and if I'm hit hard enough I could permanently lose it all. The way things were escalating, it looked like I was headed for a worse beating than the one I'd been given in elementary school.

I'll never forget the fear of seeing their angry faces so close to mine, the nearly heart-stopping anxiety of wondering how long it would take to heal from whatever beating they would give me. Then all of a sudden, BOOM! Those bullies were out of my face and against the opposite wall. I blinked in surprise. My brother Travis held the back of each tormenter's shirt balled up, one in each fist. His linebacker's grip had shoved their bodies into the metal lockers so hard they'd made dents in the doors. "If you lay one finger on my little brother," he growled, "I will have you put in jail."

It was interesting to see how quickly the bullying turned to fear. Those boys were nearly scared to death to be on the other side of the hall. After Travis pulled them off me and sent them on their way, they avoided me. He wasn't huge and green, but Travis was a bigger hero to me than the Incredible Hulk.

Unfortunately, Branson's schools caused too many problems for us. We felt like we didn't belong there. So my parents put us in a private education setting where they thought we'd be treated more fairly.

They were wrong.

"We claim the privilege of worshiping almighty God according to the dictates of our own conscience and allow all men the same privilege, let them worship how where or what they may."

— Articles of Faith, #11

Chapter 18

New Life Academy was a non-denominational Christian school that promised, "No matter what religion you come from, everyone is treated fairly." That sounded good to us. I learned a lot from our time spent in the public school system. It isn't right to shun people for having different beliefs. As long as they're not hurting anyone else, we should respect each other's right to worship as they choose. We don't have to agree in order to be friends. Sharing beliefs is fine. Trying to force them on someone else is not. No matter what walk of life someone is from, each person has the agency to believe whatever they want. No good comes from persecution.

We were surprised to find that once we enrolled in New Life Academy, and the administration realized we were Mormons, they claimed we were not a Christian religion. They treated us like outcasts. Not only did we endure verbal taunts, such as the accusation of growing horns on our heads, but we also dealt with our clothes being stolen from gym class more than once.

Everything considered, public school was worse. Besides, what else was there for us? Mother's elementary school teaching degree wasn't sufficient to home school those of us in high school, so we really had no other option than to stick it out and try to convince people in the Academy that we truly believed in Jesus Christ. It wasn't easy to persuade them. We were required to take a Bible to school every day, but they wouldn't let us take our "quads"—a combined set of all four books of scriptures sacred to us, including the Old Testament, New Testament, Book of Mormon, and Doctrine and Covenants.

I was startled one day to find our faith listed in one of the chapters of my American History class textbook under cults and false religions. So there I was, reading about my own religion listed as false. That put my young testimony on the line and my faith to the test. After class I went up to the teacher and said, "I'm a Mormon, and this book says that my religion is not true. What do you say about that?"

"I'm sorry, but this"—my teacher gave the book a firm tap with his finger—"is American history."

I said, "If you don't mind, I'd like to go home and prepare a message on who the Mormons really are and what they're about. Then I'd like to come back and present my findings to the class."

After a moment of thought, he said, "All right. Permission granted."

So I went home and spent a lot of time preparing a report. The next day I returned to class and presented my findings. I concluded with, "If you want to learn something, go to the main source of truth. To learn about math, go to a math teacher. If you truly want to learn about the Mormons, go to The Church of Jesus Christ of Latter-day Saints. Don't go to a philosopher and let him tell you about a religion that he's unfamiliar with and doesn't understand. But most importantly, if you want to know the truth of all things, go to Heavenly Father. 'If any of you lack wisdom, let him ask of God, that giveth to all men liberally and upbraideth not, and it shall be given him.' (James 1:5)." I made enough copies of my report for everyone to put in their textbooks.

During a school assembly where my brothers and I sang with the choir, I glanced at Shane, who was looking at me. It was as though an unspoken message passed between us as we both raised our hands. "Yes?" the director said.

"Could my brothers and I sing something?" Shane asked. With permission granted, we stood and sang "I Am a Child of God," a song learned in Primary, the children's organization of our church. Doing our best to harmonize, we presented the timeless words of all three verses so the audience would know without question that we were Christians who believed in God.

I am a child of God,
And He has sent me here,
Has given me an earthly home
With parents kind and dear.

I am a child of God,
And so my needs are great;
Help me to understand His words
Before it grows too late.

I am a child of God.
Rich blessings are in store,
If I but learn to do His will
I'll live with Him once more.

Lead me, guide me, walk beside me,
Help me find the way.
Teach me all that I must do
To live with Him some day.

I learned that song in Primary from the time I could talk. I also sang it at my mother's knee and whenever I felt afraid. Because I sang it so much, I didn't always think of the meaning and had come to take it for granted. At that moment, with the words soaring up to heaven and the audience's eyes blinking with tears, it hit me—the audience loved and cherished the concept that we are truly children of a loving Father in Heaven. They clung to the spiritual truth of an eternal family. The words and music stirred their souls to the point of deep hope and happiness. The song touched them so deeply that the school board decided to make "I Am A Child of God" the official school song.

We are not children of a lesser God, we are children of a loving God. We are all equal in His eyes. God is no respecter of persons and does not love anyone more than another. Just because I was born with hearing loss doesn't mean I am a lesser person in God's sight. It's simply one of my rocks to carry. Some people may appear to have more rocks than others, but each bag of rocks is for our own personal growth.

My brothers and I could have kept quiet during the school assembly. Instead, we risked more rejection by sharing our beliefs through music, which wrought a change in other people's hearts, as well as our own. As we bore our testimonies by small and simple acts, we slowly, yet steadily, informed people that we truly were Christians.

I can't even imagine a life devoid of the comfort that comes through Christ's teachings. The joy of knowing that He atoned for our sins and is available at any time through prayer is immensely reassuring in a world filled with uncertainty. It is my firm belief that any person who turns his or her life over to God will find more happiness on a day-to-day basis. When trials come—and they come to everyone—simply knowing that a loving, omniscient, all-powerful being is ready and eager to help should be enough to make every day the best day of our lives.

Our difficult times in Missouri taught us a lot about tolerance and kindness, no matter what a person believes. We need to care about others simply for being human beings. If their religious beliefs are not hurting anyone, they are free to worship as they choose. I allow that right to anyone in the world and only ask that it is granted to me in return. We made some friends in Missouri and built good relationships with other religions, helping them realize that we are Christians.

But that didn't stop New Life Academy from printing a new rulebook after we left that banned Mormons from their school.

"I believe there's an element of humor in all things."
– Gordon B. Hinckley

Chapter 19

At recess one day, the school basketball coach saw my brothers and me tossing the basketball around. "Hey, can I shoot some hoops with you guys?" he asked. We agreed, so he scrimmaged with us for awhile. When I made a shot from the free-throw line, he stopped the game and said, "Ah, Justin. Okay, you guys, let me demonstrate how to shoot." He proceeded to give us a detailed step-by-step show of shooting the basketball. Beginning with the right way to dribble, he followed with the correct way to approach the basket, then stopped to demonstrate the proper stance for a jump shot and follow-through. He shot this way a couple of times, explaining each step while we looked at each other with raised eyebrows and tried to hide our smiles.

"Hey, Coach," I called out. "Once people get the basics down, they tend to develop their own style."

"No, it doesn't work like that," he insisted. "You've got to do it the right way every time, each step in order."

"You need to allow for different personalities, heights, and body types," I insisted.

Coach shook his head. "Every successful shot is like this." He demonstrated yet again.

I smiled at him and asked, "Will you accept a challenge?"

He cocked his head. "What kind of challenge?"

I bounced the basketball once, caught it, looked him in the eye, and said, "Best out of ten shots."

"Okay," he agreed, waving his hands toward himself in invitation. "Bring it on."

He made eight out of ten.

I scored ten out of ten.

Coach stared up at the swishing basket for a moment. "Hey, guys," he said. "How would you like to be on the school basketball team?"

This was new territory for Travis because he was more of a football player at heart. When we'd run laps during basketball workouts, he'd lag behind, and I'd ask, "Are you doing okay?"

"No," he'd gasp in reply. "I'm not going to make it."

It was my turn to look out for my brother. I'd say, "Do just one more. Come on, I'll run it with you." I didn't mind doing an extra lap for Travis. He soon discovered that his lack of speed wasn't such a big problem on the court when he used me as his go-to guy. If he got the ball to me, I'd put it in the basket, and vice versa. Our teamwork made us an unbeatable basketball duo. In fact, I can only think of one time in my life when Travis beat me in a foot race. It happened during a post-graduation fishing trip to Alaska.

Travis and I were the youngest ones in the fishing group, so the older guys often gave us the task of staying behind at the water's edge to clean the fish for supper. They would swap stories at camp on top of a hill and heat up the frying pans, waiting for us to bring in the main course. It wasn't technically fair, but I was so excited to be in that vast and beautiful land that I didn't mind.

One afternoon Travis and I worked side by side on the banks of the Gulkana River outside of Anchorage, busy cleaning the many fish caught that day and cutting them into frying pan sized fillets. The sun was low in the sky, the mosquitoes were too lazy to bite much, and I was looking forward to fresh fish for supper.

Then I noticed Travis suddenly tense up. Puzzled, I glanced at his face for some explanation. It was alarming to see how unnaturally pale he was. "Did you hear that?" he asked, his lips barely moving.

"Hear what?" I asked, the hairs on the back of my neck prickling.

Travis's eyes widened as they focused on something behind me. I was so frightened to see a look of such shocked horror on his face that I wouldn't have been surprised if he had passed out on the spot.

Travis and Justin's 30 lb. King Salmon

Worried, I turned to see what he was looking at. A huge bear reared up on his hind legs and sniffed the air a mere thirty yards from where we sat. Travis and I must have smelled like a couple of giant pink salmon, since we were elbow-deep in them. The bear opened his mouth, and I was on my feet in an instant. There was no question I could outrun my brother, since I was an all-star soccer player and he was an all-state football linebacker. But someone forgot to tell him that. We tore up the hill toward camp as fast as we could, running for our lives. It was surreal. For the first time since I could remember, Travis took the lead and stayed there.

When we reached camp, we gasped out the news that we had just escaped from a bear. One grizzled old guy in a red baseball hat tipped the brim of his cap up and gave me a dubious look. "It could have been a dog," he said.

"No, sir," I replied, while Travis bent over with his hands on his knees, panting for air.

"That . . . was . . . no . . . dog," Travis insisted.

The men did not seem to take us seriously. One said, "You two get back there and get those fish." Needless to say, we were not eager to go. Eventually they gave us some bear repellent spray and convinced us to return. "That's our supper," one man said. "Just man up and you'll be fine."

Out-numbered and out-argued, we returned. Slowly cresting the hill, we looked for any sign of the bear. We didn't see him, but it was obvious that he'd wiped out about half the catch, including the fish we had already cleaned. There was barely enough left over for supper. We scooped them up and dashed back to camp.

I'm glad Travis was looking out for me. If he hadn't heard the bear growl and warned me of danger I couldn't hear, I may have sat there cleaning fish until I became the bear's entrée.

What's ironic about this whole thing is that I began collecting bears when I turned twenty-one.

"We are all, it seems, saving ourselves for the senior prom but many of us forget that somewhere along the way we must learn to dance."

– Alan Harrington

Chapter 20

M oving to Sanpete County, Utah, was one of the greatest events in our lives. We had to leave Father behind to continue work in Branson, but every chance he got, he'd come home to the Rocky Mountains to be with family. The mountains of Utah are dear to our hearts. We're country folks who love camping, fishing, hunting, the mountains, and everything to do with the outdoors.

When we got back to Utah, we turned our Fairview ranch into our primary residence. I took my younger siblings—especially Troy—on many four wheeler rides through the beautiful mountains and lush aspen groves and foothills surrounding our valley home. Today, my favorite thing to do is take my nieces and nephews on four wheeler rides up in the mountains. I think that's why I'm their favorite uncle!

In keeping with my tradition of going to a new high school every year, I started my Senior year at North Sanpete High. It was like heaven. No one tried to run us out. Even though I hadn't grown up with those kids, I made friends quickly. One other thing that soon became apparent was, for good or bad, people know a lot more about you in a small town.

I had a lot of fun my senior year. Not only was I on the football team, but I became the Sterling Scholar in music and was voted as "The Most Preferred Man." That was rather ironic, since I was also

Justin, Keaton, Aspen, and Andelyn on 4-wheeler

voted "The Most Shy Person" my junior year. I attribute that title to my hearing loss. I usually felt left out in groups because I couldn't understand everything. I felt more involved in crowds when my brothers were around, because they'd repeat what was said if necessary so I could make informed comments. I was always more comfortable with my family close by.

I never had a girlfriend in high school because I was truly shy. Dating was very difficult. I especially worried about missing out on conversations. If I didn't know what was said, how would I know how to respond? Sometimes Shane and I would put together a group date. We always looked for places that weren't too loud, because I didn't want to have to ask my date, "What? What?" after every comment she made. We thought that watching a movie in a theater might be safe, but it turned out that I couldn't follow what was going on. Actors don't always face the camera, so I couldn't read their lips. Since I'm so used to asking questions when I don't understand something, I leaned over and asked Shane what the characters were saying. He tried whispering an answer in my ear, but to me, whispers are no better than silence. In the darkness, I couldn't read Shane's lips. At last I decided not to disrupt the other movie-goers and just sat in the darkness trying to understand the movie the best I could.

Afterward, I would ask, "All right, what was going on in there?" Shane did most of the explaining, and I'd throw questions out until I was satisfied that I understood the main storyline. I definitely prefer watching DVDs with subtitles.

One dating activity I truly enjoy is dancing. In fact, I love, love, love to dance! Where do you think Donny and Marie got their moves for "Dancing With The Stars?" Despite my love for dancing, I had a challenge attached to it. I'd go to school dances where everybody screamed, yelled, and sang. I'd be dancing away with my dance partner, but if she said something in the dimly lit school gymnasium, more than half the time, I wouldn't be able to understand her. I despised saying, "What?" or "Huh?" but found myself saying them so many times it was embarrassing. If I didn't get what she said the third time, I just gave up and guessed. I'd respond with what I hoped was the right thing to say. This kind of scenario creates communication gaps between people. If you can't communicate, how do you draw closer together?

Another issue regarding school dances was that I hardly ever knew what song was playing. I may have been familiar with the tune, but I would never get all the lyrics. On the dance floor, I could hear the music, but couldn't quite understand the words, so how could I dance to it? Usually I'd feel the vibration of the bass or drumbeat, and that's what kept me going. Many times I was embarrassed to find myself still dancing when the music stopped. That's me, dancing away with no music—and it's happened quite a few times. The main reason for this is the noise mix of people screaming, yelling, and talking outweighs the music.

I think everyone would benefit from taking time to converse in quiet areas. There's nothing wrong with watching movies, but if that's all you ever do, you don't really know what the other person is like. You only get an idea of what kind of movies they enjoy.

I think it would be wise if we were all more sensitive in communicating with one another. Similar to what I wrote in Chapter Three, closeness is a matter of communication, and communication is a matter of understanding. If we really want to draw close to someone, we need to effectively communicate with them. If we want to communicate with them, we need to understand the situation they're in. In my case, it would have been more convenient if my dates understood what I was going through.

All the young ladies I have gone out with have been very kind and understanding, even when I took time to adjust my car mirrors. I often tilted the rear-view mirror so I could see my date's lips—not because I wanted to see her luscious lips (well, okay, that was nice, too), but simply so I could understand what she was saying. It worked quite well until the sun went down and I could no longer read her lips.

Yet in spite of my best efforts, I still found myself in embarrassing situations.

Recently, I picked up a date, and we headed out of the countryside enroute to the city. I signaled for the freeway onramp and merged into traffic. I thought things were going rather well. She was pleasant company, and I enjoyed talking to her. Yet something changed after we merged onto the freeway. She was suddenly quiet. I made a comment, and she gave a short answer. I couldn't help wondering what might be wrong. Was the temperature in the car uncomfortable for her? I asked, but she assured me she was fine. I fell silent myself, mulling over the possibilities. Had I said anything offensive? If so, how could I find out what it was without being even more distasteful? Maybe it wasn't anything I said. Maybe it was something else entirely. Did I have bad breath? Had my deodorant quit working?

Finally, the young lady leaned over and gently touched my shoulder. Maybe there was nothing wrong after all. Perhaps her silence was because she was building up courage to whisper sweet nothings into my ear. Maybe she was waiting for me to make a move. With a million thoughts racing through my mind, I said, "Yes?" with my heart pumping like crazy. What was she going to say?

She leaned closer, her mouth so close that her breath tickled my ear. "Are you going to turn the blinker off?"

I was so embarrassed my face turned three shades of red—rose, sunset, and dead center of the bonfire. I remembered watching other cars rolling along with their blinkers going and no turn in sight. "Well," I'd tell myself, "they'll have to turn, sooner or later." Then I drove on past, feeling a bit superior to those clueless drivers.

Now I had joined the dreaded Blinker Brigade, without enough sense to turn off the blinker when it was no longer needed.

Once the annoying blinker was taken care of, my date opened up again. We shared some personal experiences and some laughter. We arrived at our destination in good spirits, had some dinner, took in a show, then headed back home.

I wish I could tell you this story had a happy ending, but the terrible truth is, I did it again. After merging onto the freeway, I didn't think twice about that blasted blinker, but drove along in blissful ignorance until my date tapped my shoulder again.

"What?" I asked, thinking she might tell me what she liked best about the date, perhaps thank me for taking her out for a marvelous night on the town, and that she was enjoying herself ever so much.

"Are you going to turn that stupid thing off?" she asked, pointing to the little green arrow on my dashboard display . . . *blink* . . . *blink* . . . *blink* . . . *blink* . . . . I was nearly hypnotized by the monotonous flashes, but recovered myself enough to click the lever to "off."

I was certainly "off" that night. She got to see a side of me that I don't voluntarily show people, and it was purely by accident. I can really only think of one thing worse: being on a date, having fun getting to know each other through great conversation, when all of a sudden, the hearing aid battery goes dead.

Spare hearing aid batteries are like clothing to me. I always wear some in my pocket. Yet there have been times when I was in such a hurry that I wasn't thinking things through to the end and may have changed clothes without transferring batteries. All of a sudden, one ear is dead to the world, and I'm struggling to listen with half my hearing. What makes it even worse is reaching into my pocket to grab some batteries and not finding any.

Awkward.

I just keep talking, acting as if nothing has happened, straining to catch what my date is saying, and doing my best to read her lips. Then, just when it couldn't possibly get any worse, the other hearing aid goes dead. Now I'm in sudden panic. I'm sitting across from a girl I really like, and I've suddenly entered a world of complete silence.

Now I'm desperately trying to read her lips and not getting everything she's saying. So, do I risk making a fool of myself and play the guessing game? Or do I stop the conversation and tell her, "I'm sorry, I can't hear you at all. My batteries just went dead, and I can't hear a thing. Would you write out everything you want to tell me on this napkin here? Oh . . . no pen? That's all right, just use your straw and write in root beer."

This has happened on more than one date. Most of the time the girls truly did not know how to react, but did their best to be as understanding as they possibly could. They didn't want to put me in an uncomfortable situation, but I was already in one. There wasn't much they could do, unless they whipped out their hands and started signing to me. That didn't happen.

Dating has presented some really tough challenges for me. I know I am far from perfect and I have so much to learn. I try to maintain an open mind/heart so that I can learn, be better, and grow from the everyday lessons that come my way. Although I am still single, my utmost desire is to unite with my best friend and sweetheart very soon.

In similar situations, I've even lost my hearing aid battery power during school. I might be looking at the professor, studying his lips to catch every word, when my hearing batteries suddenly die. It only takes thirty seconds to replace them, but that's thirty seconds of lecture I miss.

Now imagine being on stage, speaking to hundreds of people, when suddenly your hearing aid batteries give out. First of all, you can't change your battery when you're in the spotlight and people are watching and listening to you. At the same time, giving a presentation is not like conversation because, face it, I'm doing all the talking. It may be startling to be dropped into sudden silence with hundreds of eyes trained on your every facial feature and gesture, but it's not really as bad as the other scenarios because of the fact that you're not having a conversation. No one expects you to answer them or take notes for a pop quiz.

Since I've had so many episodes of hearing battery failure, you may ask why I don't put in fresh batteries every day. The thing is, though, it's not always easy to get hearing aid batteries. Usually I can buy them in any pharmacy, but they certainly aren't cheap. If the pharmacy is closed, I have to wait. In some third world-countries, batteries are impossible to find.

Battery life is dependent on the type of hearing aid. I wear very powerful instruments with a 312 battery that usually lasts four or five days.

One thing I appreciate about the new hearing aid models is that they give a little warning beep to signal that the battery is almost dead. That's so much nicer than when I was younger and all of a sudden I was dropped into silence with no warning. Now I get a couple of minutes to change my battery before it dies.

Hopefully, I'll have some spares in my pocket.

"As human beings, our greatest glory consists not of never falling but in rising every time we fall."

– Oliver Goldsmith

Chapter 21

The only drawback to attending North Sanpete High School was that they didn't have a soccer team. One day, the school's football coach came to our door asking for me. When I walked into the room, Coach Wooten introduced himself and said, "I hear you're a soccer player. Do you think you could kick for our football team?"

Throughout my school years I enjoyed all sports, my favorite being soccer. Football was a bit of a challenge because I had to wear a helmet the whole time. Helmets have been a plague to me ever since Little League football, where my jumbo hearing aids created such feedback inside the helmet that it echoed like microphones in a racquetball court. My hearing aids also made it difficult to put my helmet on and off during the game. I eventually came up with a solution. I would play without my hearing aids, and the sideline coaches came up with hand signals to let me know what I was supposed to do.

"Justin?" Mother called from the doorway. "What's this about football?" So I told her. She glanced up at Coach Wooten and said, "Please sit down." Mother sat across from him and immediately put some stipulations on my football career. "Coach, your guys need to protect Justin. If he's hit too hard, he gets bad migraine headaches. If they're bad enough, he could lose his hearing completely for a few days, if not permanently." Coach nodded solemnly. Mother leaned forward.

"The rest of the team has to keep him from getting hit, or I won't let him play."

It was kind of embarrassing to have Mother talk about me like that. If anybody understands the game of football, they know that the opposing team is not allowed to tackle the field goal kicker without a heavy penalty. I knew Mother spoke out of love, so I just shot a tough-guy smile at Coach. Coach winked at me, then turned to Mother and grinned. "I agree," he said. "The team will keep him safe."

The first time I suited up in a Hawks football uniform and pulled on the helmet, my hearing aids created terrible feedback. Inside the bubble of my helmet, the noise was maximized to a nearly intolerable decibel level. So I experimented by inserting the hearing aids through the exterior side holes of my helmet.

Some say the field goal kicker is the most traumatizing post on the team, but it was the perfect position for me. If there were thirty seconds left in the game and our team was two points down, the kicker was the one who had to make a three-point field goal attempt that decided the game. Now that's pressure. When you're under pressure with screaming fans all over the place and TV cameras and radio announcers and bands playing and the opposing team trying to distract you, it's almost more than a body can take. So, as always, I found a solution. I took my hearing aids out. The absolute silence gave me total focus. It was just me and the ball. When I was in that state of mind, more often than not my kick tipped the score with the winning points in the game. Let me tell you, that was the best feeling in the world.

Another sport I really liked was track. My favorite event was the two-mile long distance run. No matter what sport I was involved in, the best thing about playing was having my family at the games. My family encouraged me and pumped me up to play my best. "Whenever you move out onto the field, all the parents scream and yell!" Mother would say. "They know things are going to happen when you're out there, Justin!"

I appreciate all the times my mother and brothers and sisters watched from the stands, but one special day Father joined them. For the first time, he would see me run a high school track event. I always did my best, but this day I put my whole heart and soul into preparation.

When I got out on the track, I searched the stands until I found Father pointing a video camera my way. Mother sat beside him, smiling, waving, and yelling. You could never miss my mother in the crowd because she was always the loudest and made up crazy cheers! She must have carried over the enthusiasm from her BYU cheerleading days. My heart surged with excitement to see them there. I wanted to win that race and make them proud.

A two mile run is eight laps around the track. I took my position, feeling good about the hard work I'd done to be in top shape. I was focused and ready to take off running. At the crack of the starting gun, I dashed down the track. From the moment I left the starting blocks, I was in the lead and held it easily around the first curve. My feet were so light I felt like I was flying. By my fourth lap, I was still in the lead, feeling so proud, knowing Father was taping my victory.

Then something totally unexpected happened. I still can't explain it. For some strange reason, my body started giving out. It felt like I hit some kind of invisible wall that slowed me down. It was so frustrating to feel myself run slower and slower until runners started passing me. I couldn't believe it. Like a bad dream, my legs resisted going faster, as though slogging through thick mud. If that wasn't bad enough, I was slowed even more by sudden stomach pain as sharp as a dagger. It didn't make any sense. I was an experienced runner, I knew about pacing, and this shouldn't have happened. By the eighth lap, I was behind all the other runners, but I kept on going until I crossed the finish line in last place.

I dragged myself to the sidelines and began post-race stretching with a heavy heart. Father still had his camera trained on me, and I was in so much pain, I just wanted to hide. I was so angry at myself for losing steam and coming in last place, but more than anything, I was embarrassed. I kept my head down, trying to figure out how I could possibly have ended in last place. Father has always inspired me to do my best and be a winner, not a quitter, and now I'd blown the perfect opportunity to show him I could win.

As my mind was going a hundred miles an hour trying to think of what I was going to say to my father, I saw him walking toward me. I didn't meet his gaze, but when I couldn't put off eye contact any longer, I looked up to see the biggest smile on his face. He sat beside me and did what he always did. He put his arm around me in a warm hug.

"Father," I said, my eyes dropping to the ground. "I'm sorry I didn't win this race for you."

In his quiet way, he answered, "You finished the race, son. Because of that, you made me the proudest father I could ever be. It's not always about winning or coming in first or second or third place, or even last place. The fact is, you never gave up. In the race of life, it's not about ending up in first place, it's about finishing the race."

Father's words made me feel so much better that I was able to hold my head high. He'd taught me yet another great lesson. Don't be totally focused on the problem. Avoid putting yourself in a "poor me" scenario. When people have troubles, they tend to beat themselves up too much and get depressed. Each person can make the call to pick themselves up. You are the only one who can make a lasting difference in your life. Don't expect others to do it for you. It's not always about winning. It's about giving the best you have until it's over.

"Be who you are and say what you feel because those who mind don't matter and those who matter don't mind."

— *Dr. Seuss*

Chapter 22

I'll be forever grateful to my parents for helping us enjoy the outdoors. I think our love for hunting and camping generated from my mother's side of the family, which blossomed to a higher level by Travis. We camped a lot just for fun. While in the mountains, I often took my younger siblings on four-wheeler rides, bumping along the mountain trails and reveling in the beauty of God's earth.

It was Father who took us on our first deer hunt. I know that some people don't agree with hunting. I value their opinion and want to make it perfectly clear that I respect the sanctity of life. I believe in wildlife management, which is a humane way of reducing herd sizes so that animals in the wild don't starve to death. By making a quick, clean shot, an animal is culled from the herd, leaving room for other animals to graze and grow. When I hunt, I use what I harvest. I eat the meat, just as a non-hunter might eat a hamburger from a fast food restaurant.

The difference is the person with the hamburger did not shoot the cow they're eating. It's the same with fish sticks or a chicken Cobb salad. If you're eating meat, you're really in the same boat I am as a hunter. You just skipped a step.

The only thing that could improve hunting for me is if I could hear better. For example, my brothers can locate game by listening to movement through the trees or hearing the high, eerie bugle of a calling elk.

On one memorable hunt, I was carrying a license to bag a deer. Shane went with me to help scout. Since I was the one with the tag, I led the way along a deer trail that crossed perpendicular to another game trail. Shane followed along behind, walking as quietly as he could. That's when he heard a curious sound behind him. When he turned his head, he spotted a big buck hopping down the perpendicular trail we'd just crossed. Not wanting to scare the animal into a dead run, Shane whispered, "Justin! Justin! Justin!" But I couldn't hear him. I couldn't hear the deer hooves striking the dirt, either. I just kept on walking while the deer strolled on past. I missed an opportunity because I couldn't hear.

In spite of my limitations, I have some exceptional outdoor skills. The other senses have fine-tuned enough to make me a mighty hunter within the family. My eyesight is phenomenal. If we hunker down to scan for game, I use my eagle eyes to point out animals on a far hillside that Travis, Shane, or Troy struggle to find through binoculars. When it boils down to ability, they're my ears and I'm their eyes. All of my brothers swear that I have the uncanny ability to somehow sense animals out in the wild. It may be that I'm so used to living in silence that I can sneak through the woods like no other.

When we hunted together as teenagers, nothing spurred Travis's anxiety more than not being able to communicate with me. He liked me to be by his side, because if we got separated, I wouldn't hear anyone calling my name.

One cold October day, we were hunting elk above Fairview, Utah, at 9,000 feet. Sometimes if you have two or more hunters, splitting up is the best strategy to find game. Since we had brought a pair of radios to communicate with, Travis let me out of his sight. I was in position, scanning for game, when my radio vibrated. "Yes?" I whispered.

"You okay?" Travis's voice sounded through the speaker.

"Yeah," I answered.

Fifteen minutes later, my radio vibrated again. I rolled my eyes and answered, "Hello?"

"Do you see anything yet?"

"No. When I do, you'll hear a gunshot, okay?"

Justin and Travis with elk antlers

Fifteen minutes later I answered another radio call. Without saying so much as "Hello," I whispered, "Shhh! Quit talking so much!"

Finally, Travis quit calling. Even when it started getting dark, I didn't hear from him—which wasn't like him at all. Later, I found out that he'd called me twice to ask if we should head back, but all he got from my end was silence. Of course, his anxiety peaked. Heart racing, he fought down thoughts of me lying dead somewhere. Images of my helpless body passed out in the snow with a broken leg weren't much better. He pushed them away, concentrating on the possibility that my radio batteries had gone dead.

Travis gritted his teeth. We were surrounded by pine trees, which didn't make it very easy to locate a body. He headed through the gloom toward the area where I was supposed to be, but I wasn't there. The snow cover was so old and tramped down and scattered with debris from the trees overhead that it was impossible to follow my tracks. Besides, it was dark.

Panicked, Travis ran around looking for me, trying desperately to cover as much ground as possible. When he'd run so far he was gasping for breath, he stopped and fired three shots in the air. He stood anxiously listening, looking in every direction, but I still didn't show up. Now it was full dark, and I was nowhere to be seen. Travis kept frantically calling me on the radio, but I didn't respond. He diligently searched for me until 10:30 p.m. Then he realized there was nothing else he could do but call Sanpete Search and Rescue to report a missing deaf guy who couldn't even hear them yell.

Anxiety mounted in Travis's heart with each step he took out of the canyon. Every second counted. If I was still alive, I could be freezing to death. He had to get help, and get it now. Once he cleared the canyon rim, he jogged for the truck. As soon as he reached it, he grabbed the handle and yanked open the door, which automatically turned on the overhead light.

He gasped in disbelief as I sat up and rubbed the sleep from my eyes. Squinting at him through the glare of the interior light, I asked, "Where have you been?" It looked as though Travis wanted to give me a hug, but I think he wanted to strangle me, too. It was hard to tell. "My batteries went dead," I explained. "I couldn't call you on the radio and tell you, so when it got dark I came back to the truck." It made sense to me. I don't know why he didn't check the truck before climbing all over the mountain in the dark, but I appreciated his concern for me.

From then on, Travis refused to leave me in the outdoors unless Shane was there to act as my ears. When I think about it, I didn't even realize how much Travis had my back over the years. I couldn't have asked for a better hunting partner, guide, and outfitter.

One time Travis came up with a new solution for keeping track of me. When we went out hunting he encouraged me to take the coveted tree stand position. A tree stand is a small platform about a meter square that is set up high in a tree along a game trail. A lot of people set up tree stands and leave them there so they can go back year after year. The hunter can sit or stand on the platform to take a higher vantage point in spotting game and getting a clear shot.

Travis led me to the spot he had in mind and pointed up to the tree stand. It looked about thirty feet high. "Justin, you stay on the stand until I get back, and I'll see if I can drive a deer toward you." So I climbed, and Travis took off in another direction. He was sneaking through the trees when he suddenly heard me scream with terror. Travis whirled around and dashed back toward me. My screams were so panicked that he was afraid a bear was eating me. In reality, it was much worse. You can face off with one bear and see what you're up against, but when you've bumped a yellow jacket nest beside your tree stand and spilled out hundreds of angry yellow jackets, you can't face the enemy. They buzzed around me from every direction, stingers jabbing any exposed flesh they could find. I jumped nearly thirty feet off the tree stand in one leap and hit the ground running. Fortunately, I didn't break or sprain anything. I made a mad dash for my life with an angry cloud of yellow jackets chasing after me.

I didn't get a deer that day.

Heather remembers Mother pacing the floor one day after I took off on a solo hike to camp on a nearby mountain. Even though I'm a very capable individual and an Eagle Scout, my family still worries about me. Many people don't know that I've had a lot of close encounters with dangerous wildlife, including bears. I didn't dare tell my mother in case she would never let me go camping again.

Once I saw a pair of dead bull elk lying on the snowy ground. Curious, I walked over to investigate. It was an awe-inspiring sight, but I soon realized there was more to the scene than met the eye. I'd stumbled upon a recent kill with claw slashes of bright red raking the corpses. It was when I spotted bear scat—so fresh the steam was still rising—that the skin on the back of my neck started crawling. Even though there was not a bear in sight, I could feel beady black eyes trained on me. I imagined a dripping crimson snout sniffing the wind for my scent. It appeared that I had disturbed a bear's meal without hearing a single sound from the retreating 600-pound animal. I thought he may have been keeping his distance for the time being, but how long would it take for him to decide I'd make a tasty two-legged dessert? I felt my body tense as though bracing itself for sharp curved claws poised only inches from my flesh. I backed away from the elk, my eyes scanning the trees around the clearing. As soon as it seemed safe, I turned and hightailed it out of there.

"Great works are performed not by strength but by perseverance."

— *Samuel Johnson*

Chapter 23

That brush with a bear was not enough to keep me out of the mountains. With Travis out of the home, I was now the big brother and assumed the role of Shane's protector on an elk hunt. We were after spike bull elk and had been out for several days when we saw a herd of elk on the mountain below us. We got off our horses and tied them to a tree. Then I went right, and Shane veered down the mountainside toward the left.

No matter where I looked, there was no sign of those elk. They can move pretty fast when they want to, and I figured we'd spooked them out of the area. By the time I reached that conclusion, I'd been separated from Shane long enough that I began to worry. So I called his name. I called and called and called until I finally spotted him stalking toward me down a game trail. I was so relieved to see him safe and sound that it came as quite a shock when he threw his hat at me.

"What's wrong?" I asked.

"I was sitting in high weeds, and the elk were bedding down no more than ten yards away from me!" Shane hollered. "I was so close, I could set my crosshairs on any one I wanted. There were hundreds of elk legs beneath the trees, all moving toward me, bugling to each other with no clue I was there. My spike bull was coming in when I heard a faint noise that made the elk jump and run. I was so frustrated, Justin, because this was my chance to finally get an elk before any of my big brothers. But no; when I stood up I heard you calling, 'Shane! Shane!'"

I felt so bad about ruining his hunt, even though I did it because I was worried about him. We learned a valuable lesson that day to never yell on a hunt. Now we always use our radios.

Shane and Justin outdoors

I recently had the opportunity of a once-in-a-lifetime big bull elk hunt. Travis and two of my buddies, McKade Cook and Gabe Eckertt, joined me. Travis went out of his way for me and guided us to a rugged mountain range where he had scouted earlier. We were at 10,000 feet, glassing the ridges as far as we could see, but nothing we saw fit my expectations. After searching, hiking, and sweating until 4:00 p.m., we finally found a bull elk worth pursuing. He was a couple of miles away and we only had two hours of daylight left. My gang looked at me and asked if I wanted to take the risk and go after this bull, knowing it would be one heck of a horrendous hike in the short amount of time before sunset. I didn't even think twice when I said, "Let's go get that Mack Daddy!"

It was the most exciting chase of my life. After we started the long hike to reach the big bull, we came across fifteen more bulls. Every one was smaller than the one I was after, but still big enough to be tempting. A few times I placed my scope cross hairs on the animal, finger on the trigger, debating whether or not I should shoot. But my brother encouraged me to keep going. I would move on hesitantly, knowing that my hunt could have ended right then and there, but deep down inside I knew that my big trophy was just around the next aspen. I told myself that after going that far, I might as well keep going. My heart was beating faster as I drew closer to my target. When we were about 1,000 yards away, we glassed the elk and saw him grazing on top of the vast skyline beside a smaller bull.

We crept around to 500 yards, then slowly made our way over the ridge to a pine tree that stood between the elk and us. I got down on my stomach and put my gun on the bipod for a dead rest, setting it to "fire." McKade said the target was 380 yards, so I adjusted the scope dial to exactly 380 yards.

I can't begin to tell you how breathtaking it was when I got that majestic bull in my cross hairs. I was literally on the verge of tears. After twelve years of hoping, wishing, waiting, searching, sweating, and praying, it all finally boiled down to this very intense moment. It was the most terrifying, yet exhilarating, moment of my life. I knew that I would never come across a dream bull like that ever again, and that it was now or never. Imagine the pressure.

Travis and Justin with trophy elk

Travis kept saying, "Squeeze the trigger," while I was trying to maintain my cool and not let elk fever get the worst of me. Elk fever is not a real disease, but a condition caused by over excitement of being close to bagging the game you're after. A lot of times it has messed up the hunt of an over-excited marksman. So I turned my hearing aids off and made sure I was as calm as I could be under the circumstances, before I slowly squeezed the trigger on my 300 Winchester Mag.

The next thing I knew, my brother grabbed me and began slapping me on the back. In an out-of-control fit of excitement he exclaimed, "You hit it!"

I quickly chambered another round in case I needed to make sure my target was completely down, but he was not moving a muscle. I was delighted that I'd made a humane kill, quick and clean. For the next five minutes my buddies celebrated with me. One of the greatest dreams of my life had finally come to pass. I'd like to personally express my sincere gratitude to Travis for going above and beyond his call of duty. If it weren't for his brotherly guidance and direction, I wouldn't have all these elk steaks and jerky in my freezer right now.

Even if I hadn't harvested an elk or seen an animal on that trip, the mountains always give me a chance to immerse myself with nature. In the quiet of the countryside I can hear with my heart and feel Heavenly Father's love. Everything seems more peaceful and serene because in the vastness of God's glorious creations, all my troubles appear smaller.

Justin fishing

When the world says, "Give up," hope whispers, "Do it one more time."

Chapter 24

Another hero of mine is the animated cartoon character Scrat. He's the little squirrely guy in the movie, "Ice Age." The reason he's my hero is because he never gives up on that acorn. Whatever he has to do, whatever it takes to get it, he never gives up. Likewise, whatever our dream is, let us go after it like Scrat and never give up.

I can't tell you how many times in my life I've wanted to give up. More often than I care to admit, I've been on the verge of despair and feeling as though I couldn't take a single step further. There may be times when you feel as I have. Many times I have felt like a postage stamp. I get licked, depressed, stuck in a corner, and sent from place to place. But if I just stick to it, eventually I'll arrive at the right place.

Experience has taught me that we can overcome any trial or adversity that inevitably comes our way. We don't overcome it by getting our hearing back or re-attaching a leg or getting rid of scars. Many people whose bodies are whole, with every sense working perfectly, suffer from despair. We don't overcome hopelessness by fixing the ailments that come into our lives. We conquer adversity by simply not letting it control us, own us, or overcome us.

Acceptance is one way to deal with these kinds of issues. Everybody has challenges, whether physical, mental, psychological, emotional, or whatever they might be. Troy stands as a shining example to me of someone who's dealt with more trials than just about anyone else I know. He simply doesn't give up. I've enjoyed every minute we've spent together in the outdoors, fishing under a canopy of leaves in a blue mountain lake while engaging in deep conversation about our lives. He has so much to offer, and what's even more impressive is that he's willing to put himself out and work toward his goals in spite of challenges with depression, fibromyalgia, back surgeries, and several other ailments. Instead of focusing on his own trials, he takes nursing classes so he can go out and help other people. He truly emulates the spirit of forgetting yourself in the service of others.

"Troy inspires me because, even though he didn't ask for these challenges in his life, he has accepted them and continues to move forward."

"The most miserable people I know are those who are obsessed with themselves; the happiest people I know are those who lose themselves in the service of others . . . . By and large, I have come to see that if we complain about life, it is because we are thinking only of ourselves." — Gordon B. Hinckley

The moment you choose acceptance, you feel better about yourself. Never let challenges control your life or dictate how you feel. Don't let sorrow or regret consume every waking moment. You have better things to do.

If you must think about the problem, try turning it around in your mind. What can you change in your perspective that will give you a different view of the situation? Think about it from every angle, and let yourself appreciate any small perks that your situation may offer. For example, a broken leg might allow you to slow down and get more rest. A fender bender might allow you to walk places you need to go, giving you the benefit of exercise. Because of my hearing loss, I was allowed to take as long as I wanted on the SAT or ACT tests, which normally have strict time limits to complete. That really helped because I could read the questions more thoroughly.

Don't let your limitations keep you from going after things you want in life. When I decided I wanted to become an Eagle Scout, I not only had to complete the requirements for various merit badges, but also implement a service project approved by the Eagle Board of Review. In thinking about what I could do to serve, I thought of my dear friend, Robert, who was also hearing impaired. He was a Boy Scout, too. In fact, we were alike in many ways except that he came from a financially poor background. So I decided to raise enough money to help my friend get new hearing aids that he desperately needed.

As soon as my project was approved, I began knocking on doors and making phone calls. Orchestrating such a huge campaign took time, but it was all worth it when we ultimately brought in enough money to buy the hearing aids. I was overjoyed to have so much help in reaching this goal.

I decided that I wanted it to be a surprise. It was so exciting that it was hard to keep the secret, but I managed to tell Robert to simply wear his scout uniform and meet me at my audiologist's office. Robert didn't know what it was all about, and I wouldn't tell him. He agreed to come anyway.

So on the big day, his mother drove him to the appointment. I'll never forget the look of puzzlement on Robert's face when he stepped through the door. I waited for him and his mother to be seated, then handed Robert a box. When he opened it, he saw a pair of brand new, state-of-the-art hearing aids that he could only have dreamed of owning. He stared at them for a moment before tears started rolling down his cheeks. He was at a complete loss for words, but his tears said enough.

Justin and Robert

My audiologist led Robert to a chair so he could custom fit the hearing aids for my friend. Robert couldn't stop smiling. He thanked me over and over again. I told him it wasn't just me; I had a lot of help from a lot of generous people. His tearful mother hugged me before they left, and Robert walked away with a spring in his step. He turned his head this way and that to test the latest sounds coming through those wondrous new devices. He was hearing better than ever.

The change that came over my friend Robert that day changed my life. Since a candle loses none of its light by lighting another, I decided from that moment on that I wanted to help children all around the world with the gift of better hearing. The technology was available, and the deaf community was ready. They just needed to be matched up. In order to do that, I felt it was necessary to go to college and get the degree I needed to make my goal a reality. In truth, the thought of college scared me to death. *I'm deaf, I can't do this!* ran through my mind, but I refused to accept that excuse. So putting my Sterling Scholar music scholarship to use, I enrolled at Snow College in Ephraim, Utah.

Music classes were part of my curriculum. I determined to dedicate an hour a day in the campus practice rooms to polish my viola skills. One day, just as I began to practice, a group ensemble gathered in a neighboring room. Their saxophone, trombone, and other brass instruments sounded so loudly through the curtain divider that I couldn't even hear myself think. How was I supposed to hear myself practice? I easily could have said, "This is too loud, I'm going home and calling it a day." Instead of giving up, I found a different solution. I turned my hearing aids off. In the sudden blessed silence, I put my viola up against my jawbone and played. I could hear every single note inside my head. I don't claim that I had perfect intonation that day, but in the face of seemingly insurmountable odds, I was practicing my viola, and never did I hear one peep from the musical ensemble next door.

Don't tell me any magician wouldn't wish he had something similar that he could pull out of his hat.

You can always find some kind of solution if you don't give up. I've failed many times in taking exams, even to the point of making four attempts before finally passing. What if I'd given up after three tries? It's only in the game of baseball that it's three strikes and you're out. In the game of life, you can swing as many times as you want until you hit a home run.

Where an ordinary man finds an excuse, a courageous man finds a way. I could have used the excuse that I'm deaf, that I'm a year and a half behind the other students, but I never did. I kept on studying until I hit a grand slam and was gratified to learn that I had made the college Dean's List.

Like many other students, I had to work my way through school. A scholarship only goes so far. I applied for a job at the local hotel and was surprised to receive an assignment at the front desk where I was required to answer phone calls. That was a huge challenge for me because you can't lip read over the phone. Even worse, the hotel phone was not hearing-impaired compatible. Every time it rang I got nervous. Every time I picked it up, I was scared that I wouldn't be able to hear or understand the person on the line. I always want to give my best in everything I do. When I had to talk on the phone, sometimes I'd misunderstand things. It was especially nerve wracking to take a room reservation because I had to get their name and credit card information. I can't tell you how many times I had to repeatedly ask the person for their card number. There was no way I could make a guess in this situation and hope I was close. It had to be right. Often, it took four or five times for them to read me their entire number before I got it. Most customers were frustrated because no one wants to repeat their credit card number that many times. But that's the way it was. Even though giving up seemed the easy way out, that wasn't ever an option I chose.

One early morning I set out on a much-anticipated hunt. It was a beautiful clear day, I was in good form, and was excited to be in the outdoors. My sunny outlook was quickly dashed when I had the misfortune of falling off a cliff and dropping my gun.

Okay, I know what you're thinking. Why in the world didn't I hang onto my gun, which was worth several hundred dollars? Well, you try falling off a cliff and see what you hang on to. Hopefully, you'll have your life and be thankful for it. I managed to survive with a few bruises, but my rifle and scope were banged up so bad I thought I might as well quit and go home. Nothing was going right anyway.

Almost as soon as the thought entered my head, I pushed it out. I had very limited time to hunt and would not quit until the day was over. I got busy, hurried and fixed my gun and scope the best I could, and sighted in my gun by going to the shooting range. Then I proceeded to hunt the rest of the day, ending just before sunset with the miraculous opportunity of bagging my once in a lifetime elk mentioned earlier. What if I had given up and gone home? I shudder to think, and that's why I don't give up.

Take a breather if you must, realign your target if necessary, but don't you ever, ever give up.

"Make your life a mission, not an intermission."

– Arnold Glascow

Chapter 25

I voluntarily decided to serve a two-year mission for my church. I was called to learn British Sign Language (BSL) and serve in the U.K. (United Kingdom). I had never participated in sign language before. In fact, I grew up despising sign language and wanted nothing to do with it. It was startling when people signed to me, such as the time I was eating dinner in a restaurant with my family. From the sound of my voice, the waitress figured out that I was hard of hearing and began signing. I was very uncomfortable as she made strange gestures at me and looked to my mother for direction. She turned to the waitress and said, "I'm sorry, he doesn't know sign language." The waitress, obviously shocked, dropped her hands. Mother smiled and explained, "He only knows speech." It just so happened that by the time I turned sixteen, which was the age Mother had given permission for me to learn sign language, I didn't need it and had no desire to learn it.

After discovering that I was to learn sign language, my heart sank. I went into my room and stayed there until Father came looking for me. He found me lying on my bed and sat next to me. "Son, what's the matter?"

With a hopeless heart, I said, "Father, I don't think I'm capable of doing this mission."

His voice was patient and gentle. "Why is that, son?"

"Because I have trouble hearing in crowds, and I don't even know sign language. I just can't do it." Saying the words out loud made my heart even heavier. I don't like asking people to repeat themselves because I don't want to make them uncomfortable. I don't ask people to talk slower, either. I'd rather make an educated guess at what they say than take the risk of offending them.

I thought of the difficulty my deaf friends faced with communication at church. How does a deaf person feel the spirit if they can't understand what's being said? It all seemed so overwhelming. I can't tell you how many comments I've missed during church. There have been many times when I had no idea what the speaker was talking about. At times like those, I pulled out my scriptures and did my best to be productive with my time. I may even write in my journal. If I can grasp what the topic's about, I use it to apply other concepts that I can learn and study on my own.

There is a theory that when trying to do right, evil forces may step in with dark influences to try to stop goodness from happening. Thinking this might be the case, my father gave me a blessing. Afterward, I felt a welcome surge of hope and relief. I stood and said, "I don't know how this will all work out, but the one thing I know for sure is that, according to God's will, I can do anything my heart desires."

When I went into the Missionary Training Center (MTC) to learn what I needed to know for my mission, one of the faculty led me into a separate room. He sat me down and began signing to me. "Whoa," I said, putting my hands up to stop him. "I don't understand a thing you're trying to say." Surprised, he took me back to the main room with all the other beginners. Despite some very difficult training, I ultimately had some great experiences learning British Sign Language. Now that I know it, I love it. It involves facial expression and body language to the point that it's very entertaining and exciting. This really helped me overcome my shyness. I eventually learned to appreciate sign language as a valuable communication tool—especially for people who may have no residual hearing at all. Even some who have little residual hearing prefer to sign.

Learning sign language was the final step in allowing me to fit into the deaf culture. Because of my childhood training, I am able to function in the hearing world. Because of my hearing loss and fluency in sign language, I'm able to fit completely in the deaf community. Being able to cross over the cultures has made me unique, but it has not been easy. When I was a child, it was confusing to put in hearing aids and hear so much noise, then take them out to be wrapped in silence. It took some time for my brain to sort out the difference.

I had the opportunity to establish programs for the deaf all over the United Kingdom. One day I was in Liverpool, England, having a conversation with a man on the street. He adjusted his glasses and shifted his gaze to the right side of my head where my behind-the-ear (BTE) hearing aid sat. Then he moved his head slightly and studied the hearing aid behind my left ear. It was kind of annoying to have his attention focused on the sides of my head instead of my face. I felt like waving in front of his eyes and saying, "I'm over here, buddy."

Finally he put his hand up, and I stopped talking. "Excuse me," he said, "but why are you wearing hearing aids?"

I thought it was a rather stupid question, but I answered as politely as I could, "So I can hear better."

He pushed his glasses up the bridge of his nose, smiled, and asked, "Have you ever wondered why you have a hearing loss?"

"Yeah, sure," I answered. "I've thought about that my whole life. I believe everybody has something about themselves they wish they didn't have, whether physical, mental, spiritual, or emotional. I also believe God gives us challenges to help us grow and so that his works may be manifested. So the way I see it, my hearing loss is not a weakness but a blessing, not a handicap but a strength, not a punishment but a gift. It doesn't generate feelings of anger, but rather humility and gratitude."

"No, you're completely wrong." The man shook his head solemnly. "I'll tell you why you're deaf. You can't hear because God is punishing you for something you've done wrong. Sorry to say, but that's how it is."

I was totally taken off guard. How dare he say that to me? What gave him the right to judge me? Then doubts began creeping in. All my old insecurities seemed to pile up in my heart, spilling over the top, covering my self-worth with a heavy blanket of uncertainty.

What if he was right? What if I had done something so wrong I was cursed with deafness?

Sometimes I think the world would be a better place if people could turn their hearing off against hurtful things they don't need to hear. It was too late for me to turn off my hearing aids because I'd already been influenced by his negative words.

Then I had a sudden inspiration. Raising my eyes to meet his, I said, "May I ask you a question?"

"Sure," he replied. "Just as long as you're willing to face the truth."

"I am," I responded with a slight nod of my head. "Will you please tell me why you're wearing glasses?"

He let out an exasperated breath. "Everyone knows that," he said. "So I can see better."

Cocking my head, I asked, "Have you ever wondered why you can't see very well?"

He scratched his head, then adjusted his glasses. "I never really thought about that."

"Well, then, according to your opinion and philosophies, God must have punished you for something you did wrong."

His eyes went wide. The shock on his face was priceless. At first I wondered if he might try to hit me. Then I wondered if he was having a heart attack.

Suddenly, he relaxed and began to laugh. I'd given him a great verbal punch back, if I do say so myself. He was trying to pull a mote out of my eye when he had a beam in his own. It was funny, because while he was accusing me, it didn't even occur to him that he had something less than perfect about himself. It was refreshing that when he saw things from a different perspective, we could laugh together.

This exchange reminded me of the Biblical story of the blind man. When people asked, "Who sinned? He or his parents?" Jesus answered that neither had. The man was blind so God could manifest His good works toward all humanity. May we all learn this valuable lesson.

If God physically punished me for everything I've done wrong, I wouldn't have much of a body left. I've made a lot of mistakes, and continue to do so. I daresay that's true of everyone, because nobody's perfect.

All people are equal in God's eyes, even though some may seem higher in status for reasons of wealth or power. We cannot honestly judge anyone else's position. God doesn't look at a person's title or status. He doesn't give rewards solely to those sitting highest on any kind of celestial totem pole. He measures the progress people make and what they sacrifice in order to learn and grow closer to Him. It's like the Biblical story of the widow's mite. The tiny portion she gave was everything she had, a full 100%.

After I learned to sign, people who were deaf were more anxious to communicate with me. In the deaf culture, they develop their own little world and would purposely ignore my hearing friends who also knew sign language. I can understand why. How could hearing people possibly know what a person who is deaf was going through? There's a huge gap between the cultures—bigger than it needs to be. My paradigm is that we should all come together as humanity, united in purpose and thought.

Even though a hearing person can never truly understand the deaf culture, most people who are deaf appreciate those who try to learn their language. Making an effort helps break the ice. If you're wondering who should make the first move, think about someone with no residual hearing trying to learn speech, or someone with normal hearing trying to learn sign language. Weigh out the pros and cons. The answer is fairly clear that a person with normal hearing could much more easily learn sign language.

It's not that society doesn't care about the deaf, they just don't know how to act toward them. For example, those who talk loudly with exaggerated mouth movements. This doesn't help. What helps is simple mouth gestures, creating effective communication. When kids saw me all wired up with jumbo hearing aids, they didn't know how to react to me. They didn't know whether I could hear or talk or even think straight. But once they got to know me, we got along fine. There's always going to be some form of distortion, but as people become more tolerant, patient, and understanding of other people's needs, there will be more harmony in a very diverse world.

American Sign Language (ASL) is an authentic language, just as BSL and any other form of sign language. I decided to use my newfound sign language skills to build a united front for both the deaf and hearing. I did this by producing musical sign language events. I sent an open invitation for the hearing population to come and learn about the deaf culture. It is my belief that music is a universal language that can unite everybody from all walks of life.

One of the favorite songs at these events was entitled, "His Hands." We had a whole choir in white gloves sign along with the music. It was beautiful.

After these events, we conducted workshops to answer questions regarding the deaf culture, such as, "How can people who are deaf hear an alarm clock?" The answer would be waking up to a vibrating alarm clock. It's like an earthquake every morning, and I don't like it much. When I turn my hearing aids off at night, in a sense I'm turning my brain off. The vibrating alarm clock is a wonderful, yet uncomfortable, blessing. Some people choose to have a hearing dog. Some use remedies like flashing lights for the doorbell and blinking lights or a vibrating phone. There are many different ways to resolve challenges for the deaf in our day and age.

One day, I took the opportunity of attending a motivational seminar. I sat in the front row. The speaker's words were full of such passion that I felt the force of his message go right through me like a lightning bolt. It was nearly magical the way his voice infused me with a desire to become better than I was. I listened intently as he tucked me into the palm of his hand.

Suddenly, a startling thought struck me out of nowhere. *I'm getting out of my cocoon.* It was such a bold thought that I nearly stopped breathing. Then I took in a deep breath and set my jaw. *I'm tired of my reserved mindset. My speech isn't perfect, my hearing isn't perfect, but why should that stop me? I'm going to spread my wings and be a public speaker.*

The impression was so strong, I could not resist it. I knew I had to go for it. A deaf man speaking to crowds? Sure, why not? How hard could it be?

"I am not afraid of tomorrow, for I have seen yesterday and I love today."

– Anonymous

Chapter 26

Flying is always a challenge. Arriving home from a flight and passing through all the security gates to the baggage claim is generally a much easier task than departing to wherever my final destination may be. Before boarding any particular commercial airplane, the airport security requires that all passengers remove their shoes, jacket, and any metal devices before passing through the metal detectors at the security gates. Unfortunately—and many times in all my travels—I have unwittingly set off the security alarms. As a result, I get pulled aside for closer scrutiny. When the security wand goes ballistic at my head, the airport personnel exchange puzzled glances. So I reluctantly pull out my hardware from my ears. Usually they'll look at me with the type of awe reserved for James Bond and his incredible spyware. I simply give them a patient smile, square my shoulders, nod curtly, and proceed to my next assignment.

When I flew home in 1998 after serving two years for my church in the United Kingdom, my family picked me up at the Salt Lake City Airport. After a glorious reunion and celebration with my family, I climbed into the car, anxious to get home. To my surprise, we drove right through my old stomping grounds and kept heading south. When I asked where we were going, my family smiled, but wouldn't tell me. I figured I'd find out soon enough. When we reached the center of Ephraim, the car turned left, and we pulled up in front of a house I'd never seen before. "Surprise!" they said. "Welcome home!"

My family had actually moved without giving me their forwarding address.

Merrill Osmond family vacation to Yellowstone

When we sat around and reminisced, one of the stories that surfaced happened during my senior year of high school. My strong competitive streak made me issue a challenge to Shane and Sheila for a two-on-two basketball game against Heather and me. To make it more exciting, we decided that the losing team would have to jump into the muddy horse pasture that had just been refreshed by a rainstorm the night before. I wasn't afraid of the consequence. I didn't think I'd ever have to do it since Shane had never beaten me at basketball and Sheila was only seven years old, so what could she do? Shane and Sheila were rather reluctant to agree, but I finally talked them into it. I could hardly wait to see them take a mud and horse pucky bath.

The game started out just as I expected with my team holding a healthy lead. But then, for some strange reason, Shane found his groove. He took off and made several baskets in a row. It was like he couldn't miss. He could have closed his eyes and stood on his head and still made baskets. With luck like that, he and Sheila ended up winning.

As soon as eleven-year-old Heather realized she was on the losing team, she backed away from the corral fence, declaring, "I'm not jumping in there no matter what." So I had to do the noble thing. I grabbed her and threw her in the muddy pasture where she landed with a satisfying "plop." Feeling Shane and Sheila's astonished eyes on me, I pulled off my hearing aids and handed them to Shane. Taking a running leap, I dove head-first into the quagmire. I came up covered in mud and manure. I am nothing, if not a man of my word.

Now an idea gradually grew in my mind. It had been years since the game, but Heather had never really been sorry that she hadn't followed through on her commitment to jump in the horse pasture of her own accord. In fact, she had actually complained about my saving her honor by throwing her in. So that night after Heather fell asleep, I snuck into her room and put my vibrating alarm clock under her pillow. Of course I had set it for 3 a.m. Heather screamed when she woke up to what she thought was an earthquake. After that, she never forgot to lock her bedroom door.

Heather and Justin

Before returning to college, I visited my audiologist. My whole life, I'd worn hearing aids behind the ears (BTEs), which gave me the maximum power to compensate for my hearing loss. Another reason for wearing them was for the imbedded telecoils, which help immensely with pinpoint sound tasks such as speaking on the phone. Knowing that new technology was available, I faced my doctor and asked, "Is it possible for me to have ITEs?" (In-the-Ear hearing aids.)

He looked thoughtful, then answered, "I'm sorry, Justin, but with your severe/profound hearing loss, I'm afraid you're going to have to stick with the BTE's so you can get the maximum power needed.

However, there is one place that might be able to help you. Their name is Starkey Labs, Inc."

I'd never heard of them, but soon discovered that Starkey Labs—a custom hearing product manufacturing company—was located in Eden Prairie, Minnesota. The owner, Bill Austin, brought in many people from around the world for custom fitted hearing aids. Impressed by what we learned, Mother and I made airline reservations and traveled to Minnesota

When I arrived, I was introduced to Bill—a man large in stature with a halo of white hair. When he took my hand in a warm handshake, I immediately felt at ease. In a voice strengthened by determination, he asked, "How can I help you?"

Many people would enjoy taking advantage of a young man's admission to feeling socially inadequate and give him a hard time about it. But I felt like I could trust this gentle giant.

"I'd really like an ITE hearing aid model," I confessed. "But my audiologist doesn't know of any technology that would allow that to work with my profound hearing loss."

Bill nodded, his expression full of compassion.

I clasped my hands on my knees and continued, "You see, I'm going to college, and I feel a little . . . well . . . self-conscious." I cleared my throat. "To be honest, with my past history of dating, my self-image is on the line. I want to go on dates, but with something a little more comfortable than these." I pointed to the hearing aids perched behind my ears.

"Just because it hasn't been done before doesn't mean it can't happen," Bill said with a confident nod. "The first step is a hearing test so we can see what we can do."

Only someone who has wanted something so badly will understand how Bill's words of encouragement touched my soul with a beacon of hope. Maybe—at last—I could look like any normal guy on campus. Maybe the girls—and people in general—wouldn't focus on my ears before looking into my eyes with questions I didn't know how to answer. Maybe I could enter the dating scene on a more level playing field than ever before. How would it be to have a girl consider and accept my personality before considering my deafness?

I could hardly wait.

As Bill had said, there was no particular model for my simple request. But I soon learned that Starkey had a reputation for tenacity, and Bill would not accept "no" for an answer. While Bill and his technicians worked non-stop for a few days creating a custom hearing aid just for me, Mother and I waited. I spent the time anticipating the possibility of an exciting new chapter in my life. I anxiously hoped an upgrade in my hearing gear would really jump-start my social skills and lifestyle. People are innately social and yearn for meaningful contact with other human beings.

I came to realize that all the doctors who had said I would never benefit from a smaller hearing aid obviously didn't know Bill, or his burning desire to help others with his miraculous touch. By the time I left Minnesota, Bill had outdone himself. I was delighted that he had worked his magic and even gone a step beyond what I had requested. I could hardly believe that I was ultimately fitted with a pair of CIC's (Completely-in-Canal) hearing aids. I never thought I'd see the day. They were even smaller and less conspicuous than ITEs. Starkey's nano science had produced a nearly invisible hearing aid with close to normal, human quality hearing.

Bill Austin was an instant hero in my eyes! He showed, through his endless efforts of compassion and love, that each patient is a jewel in his crown.

Not only did I make some wonderful friends at Starkey, but they kept in contact with me after I returned home. Their regular follow-up calls to see how I was doing proved that, with my new hearing aids, I was doing great! And my speech and hearing continued to improve. While playing college intramural sports, I no longer had to worry about taking my hearing aids out to keep them safe. The sweat ran around my ears, completely missing the electronic components. They were better than anything I had ever owned.

Of course, I still couldn't wear them in the tub, the shower, or when I went jet-skiing. Because of that fact, I had the fright of my life one night at a condo my family owns in Orem, Utah. Like others in my family, I sometimes use it to stay overnight during my travels. One time I arrived at the empty condo past midnight after a long, hard day. I took my hearing aids out, and, not bothering with turning on the lights, ran a nice hot bath so I could unwind and get ready to sleep.

I was just thinking it was time to get out of the tub and climb into bed when the bathroom light suddenly flicked on. My heart leaped. I wondered if I was dreaming, and hoped I was. But after I opened my eyes and sat up, I knew I was awake. The lights had somehow come on of their own accord. I was scared to death. Could it be a faulty wire? Or had a prowler followed me inside? This was a particularly unsettling thought stemming from childhood. I recalled many times when my parents were gone, someone trying to break into our house. One time some men climbed the fence when my brothers and I were outside feeding our chickens. We headed for the house at a dead run, and the men took off after us. They might have caught us if it hadn't been for our dog, a Rottweiler named Mr. T.

Now I had the unsettling feeling that someone was after me again. Had I locked the front door? I was nearly certain that I had, but I was pretty tired. Maybe I'd overlooked that one crucial detail that could be my undoing. Why, oh, why hadn't I brought my hearing aids in with me? I called out, "Hello?" trying to sound brave while my heart hammered like a soccer ball in play.

Silence. But was it really silent? Were there stealthy noises that my damaged ears could not hear? I wet my lips and tried again. "Is anyone there?"

Suddenly, the bathroom door swung open. I startled, goose bumps raising on my flesh as I stared at the darkened doorway. No one was there. This was seriously creepy. I definitely didn't want to be caught in the tub by man or ghost, so I grabbed my bathrobe and wrapped it around myself, shivering from more than just cold. I inched toward the door, wishing again for my hearing aids sitting in the bedroom. I would have liked to be warned of any footfalls coming my way. As it was, there could have been prowlers doing the macarena right behind me and I wouldn't know it. I turned my head just to check, but there was no one else standing in the bright spotlight of the bathroom light.

Facing the dark hallway, I took another step forward. As hard as I tried, I couldn't think of any logical explanation for what was happening, except that someone had come into the condo. Who was it? What did they want? Had I already scared them away? A few more hesitant steps got me to the doorway.

That's when the attack came. Someone jumped out at me from the closet. I yelled at the top of my voice before recognizing the wicked grin on Shane's face. He scared the dickens out of me. When he stopped laughing long enough to speak, he admitted that he knew I was there because my car was parked out front. He had knocked and rung the bell before using his own key to get in. When he realized I was in the tub, he figured I didn't have my hearing aids in and decided to play a heart-stopping prank on me.

Shane's spooky prank was successful only because I couldn't hear. If he had been a real burglar, it could have resulted in an even scarier ending.

I can hardly wait for the day when waterproof hearing aids are invented. I just may be first in line to get a pair.

"Let us rise up and be thankful, for if we didn't learn a lot today, at least we learned a little, and if we didn't learn a little, at least we didn't get sick, and if we got sick, at least we didn't die; so, let us all be thankful."

– Buddha

Chapter 27

I was very fond of my new hearing aids. Having them hidden inside my ears made me more confident in talking to girls and setting up fun dates with some very sweet young ladies. However, I have learned over time that my hearing loss can be more obvious than my small invincible hearing aids. I'll be honest and admit that I was a little over-sensitive to how I looked during my school years. It happens to all of us—especially when we're teenagers. The default instinct of wanting to impress our family, friends, peers, and even our dates comes naturally, as though it happens subconsciously.

Today, I can say that I'm more concerned about being able to really hear and understand what's happening around me. The shape, form, and figure of any hearing aid wouldn't bother me as much now, as long as it was able to help me not only to hear, but to understand the precious sounds of life. I just sincerely hope that with whatever hardware I'm wearing, I am accepted for who I am and not what I am.

I'm the type of guy who'll take a table up in the canyon with a white tablecloth and have my sister and brother serve dinner for my date and me under the aspen trees. (Yeah, my siblings are really that cool!) Another time I took a girl to a nice restaurant. At the end of the meal, I pulled out my violin and serenaded her. Travis wouldn't be caught dead serenading. I have my own style, and I'm not afraid to use it.

But in reality, it's okay to be different. Just be true to yourself.

My good friend Steve Thurman and I have been on several double dates together. One especially memorable group date, we attended country singer Neil McCoy's concert. Our seats were about ten rows from the stage. In the middle of the show, Neil McCoy began singing a song with a powerful beat. I thought it would be fun to dance, so I pulled my date up to her feet, and we began dancing in the aisle. Was I self-conscious? No. I was just having fun.

Suddenly, I heard Neil McCoy call from the stage. "Hey, that guy should keep on dancing, dude!" With his encouragement, I stepped it up a little. It made me happy to see the delighted smiles on the faces around us.

After the concert, Steve pulled me aside and asked, "Did you understand what Neil said?" His face was so serious that I began to wonder if I'd made a real blunder. I knew Steve would be honest with me. The problem was, did I really want to find out what Neil said? If I ignored Steve, I could go on believing that I was as good as one of Neil's backup singers, only in the dancing department. If not . . . well . . . what had he really said? With some trepidation, I asked, "Didn't he comment on my great dance moves?"

"No," Steve answered. "He said, 'Hey, that guy looks like Donny Osmond!'"

Laughing, I admitted, "I thought he said, 'Keep on dancing, dude!'"

When all is said and done, I just try to have fun with whatever situation I find myself in, and always look for the joy.

I'll admit that I've had some difficult dating situations in which people have shown prejudice against me for my hearing loss. One young lady I had befriended invited me on an outing to "The Narrows" in Zion National Park with a group of students from school. I really liked the girl, and she seemed to like me, too. I was delighted to go along and get to know her better. While hiking through some of the most magnificent country in the world, with green trees backed by red rocks in natural formations depicting the wonders of nature, one of the young men in the group got close enough to see the tiny filament I use to remove my hearing aids. "Hey," he sneered, "you've got a bug in your ear."

I don't know if he was trying to be funny, but his comment pierced deep wounds inside. I didn't say anything. I've discovered that ignoring insensitive comments is the quickest way to make them stop. Worse than what the young man said, though, was the girl at my side growing suddenly quiet. When I tried speaking with her, she only gave short answers and refused to look at me. Not long afterward, she moved away to join another group of hikers. I could tell she was avoiding me and could only guess that her opinion had been swayed by a single thoughtless comment. She would never discuss the trip with me afterward. In fact, she continued to steer clear of me, striking another blow to my self-esteem.

Back on campus, I put the incident behind me. I hit the books and eventually earned my Bachelor's degree in marketing from Utah State University (USU). That's when I met a significant person from my past. Dr. Ted Tedeschi, one of the audiologists who first diagnosed my hearing loss, appeared twenty years after we first met. His son-in-law graduated from Utah State University the same time I did, and we became reacquainted.

He was extremely happy to see how well I had done in my life—especially in the field of communication. I'd far exceeded his expectations, and it was fun to see his reaction to my ability to speak. He attributes my success not only to my determined personality and dedication to purpose, but he also recognized the love and care I received from my parents and family with hours of speech therapy, hearing therapy, and hearing aids.

What was most exciting about talking to Tom was discovering that from his professional point of view, with the right support, the level of communication I have reached can be duplicated in other people with hearing impairments. Of course, my public speaking is more of a personality thing. It's what I love to do—captivating audiences with my story and holding a thousand people in the palm of my hand. It works because I believe in what I do, and because I love people. I appreciate Tom for his unwavering friendship, sound advice, endless encouragement, and his continued motivation to inspire me to be the best I can be.

Once I had my Bachelor's degree, it was time to join the other graduates in looking for a job. A few opportunities came my way. I worked as a public speaker and youth counselor for EFY (Especially For Youth)—a program that helps inspire young people to feel good about themselves and make good choices for their lives. That was where

I met another great friend, Rob Shirley, a fellow EFY speaker from Rexburg, Idaho.

Rob asked me if girls were ever attracted to me just because my name was Osmond. Unfortunately, that has sometimes been the case. Then Rob quickly assured me that he liked me, even before he knew who I was. This is when I can determine who my real friends are, that they accept me for who I am and not what I am.

I really enjoyed my work with EFY. I'm grateful for the chance I had to speak to thousands of kids across the country about hearing with my heart, overcoming challenges, and letting their own spirits guide them. Even though this was what I'd aspired to do, it seemed unreal that I was a public speaker. Who would think that a man with my level of hearing loss would ever speak fluently, let alone become a professional public speaker?

Yet the Starkey Hearing Foundation was still in the back of my mind. After a couple of years with EFY, I got back in touch with Starkey. Bill Austin was already a hero of mine, but my level of respect for him quadrupled for a whole new reason. I was awed by his generosity in coordinating distribution of hearing aids, not only to people in the United States, but to those in other countries worldwide. I loved the idea of giving on such a broad scale. Bill not only leads this worldwide effort through his extraordinary vision and compassion, he also voluntarily goes on each and every one of these humanitarian missions and personally fits every child with new hearing devices. His worldwide humanitarian outreach program was so impressive that I instantly wanted to align myself with Bill and become a part of this wonderful organization. I was extremely grateful that he had given me the gift of better hearing, but after observing his work of art and his true passion, I saw this as as an opportunity for me to turn around and help give that same gift to others—similar to my Eagle Scout project, only on a much greater scale.

I gathered my courage and called the Starkey Hearing Foundation to ask about a job. I humbly admit that Bill has touched my life substantially—in more ways than one—especially when he offered me employment on a three-month trial basis. Because of the incredible service and generosity that the Starkey Hearing Foundation provides, my three months turned into more than ten years of working under his inspired direction.

The opportunities Bill has given me have dramatically touched my life in many different ways. Without Starkey's role in spearheading my career, I would not be traveling the globe to help expand their worldwide hearing aid distribution programs. Today, I am very humbled to play a small part in helping build the Starkey Hearing Foundation into one of the world's largest outreach programs, distributing more than 100,000 hearing aids every year in more than 85 different countries—some that even have elephants.

Justin riding an elephant in India

Every humanitarian hearing mission is sponsored by generous individuals, corporations, doctors, hearing specialists, businesses, civic organizations, and many other donors who come together on a volunteer basis to make these events possible. With their generous help, we supply batteries, hearing aids, ear molds, and everything else we need to get the job done.

Over the years, I have to look back and thank Bill Austin for the abundance of amazing experiences and opportunities that he has given me. Thanks to his generosity in allowing me to travel the world, I've had some pretty crazy things happen that I wouldn't experience any other way. My sister Heather remembers a crisp autumn day when I sent her a text message saying that I'd just eaten a guinea pig in Peru for Thanksgiving.

Justin and young boy with new hearing aids.
"Thumbs up! I can hear!"

I currently serve in public relations, as a board member, and the spokesperson for the Starkey Hearing Foundation. I speak at conventions, workshops, trade shows, luncheons, and seminars, giving keynote speeches to promote our cause. Like many other service-oriented jobs around the world, I am grateful for the opportunities to serve and help others hear. I'm just happy to play a small part in making a big difference, for which I don't take any credit. When you find a job you like, it seems like you never have to work a day in your life.

I spend a considerable amount of time promoting hearing awareness programs, such as the Starkey Hearing Foundation's annual "So the World May Hear" gala. We raise millions of dollars to benefit children around the world with the gift of better hearing, bringing in special guests like Elton John, Larry King, Jay Leno, Bill Clinton, Muhammad Ali, my crazy Uncle Donny, and many others who so generously utilize their time and resources to give back to those in need. I enjoy serving with these wonderful, generous, yet down-to-earth common-folk people. I try to keep in mind that together we can help provide the greatest gift in helping those who can't help themselves.

Singer Trisha Yearwood, Justin, and singer Garth Brooks

Singer Gladys Knight with Justin

Actor Brendan Fraser and Justin

Justin with comedian Billy Crystal

Actress Jane Seymour and Justin

Justin with baseball Hall of Famer Willie Mays

Justin and actor Kurt Russell

Justin and actress Goldie Hawn

"America's Got Talent" judge Sharon Osbourne and Justin

Justin with Troy Aikman of Dallas Cowboys football team

Justin and golf Hall of Famer Arnold Palmer

Justin with basketball star Magic Johnson of the L.A. Lakers

Justin and actor Chuck Norris

Justin and Ty Pennington of "Extreme Makeover: Home Edition"

Nascar driver Richard Petty and Justin

Justin with comedian Dick Van Dyke

Warren Buffet giving his wallet to Justin

Justin with NRA (National Rifle Association)
Executive Vice President Wayne Lapierre

With my background in the entertainment business, I've learned that people are just people, no matter what they do for a living. We are all equal in God's eyes. The guy whose face is on every billboard has bad breath in the morning, too. The only difference is, he has to use a billboard-sized bottle of mouthwash.

On one of my travels, I was checking out of a hotel room when a woman asked, "Where are you from?"

"Utah."

My answer took her by surprise. She thought I was from outside of the United States because of the slight deaf accent to my speech. I try hard to perfect my speech and communication so I can fit into the normal crowd, but that will always be a challenge for me.

Because I have difficulty pronouncing the "s" sound, I sometimes pronounce my name indistinctly. One time a radio host misunderstood my name and said into the microphone, "Today we'd like to welcome Jason Ormond to our show."

I said, "It's good to be here, but just so you know, my name is Justin Osmond."

"Sorry," he said, "We're glad to have you, Justin." Then he proceeded with a five minute interview on the Starkey Hearing Foundation. At the end of the interview, he said, "Thanks for being here, Justin Ormond."

Justin and Mary Osmond showing the "I love you" symbol with three Colombian brothers who are all deaf

I said, "Thank you, but again, my name is Justin Osmond, of the Osmond family."

There was a five second pause. Then the interviewer's voice sounded quietly. "I am so sorry, Mr. Osmond."

This honest mistake may have been avoided if I could only pronounce my esses right.

Steve still gives me a hard time regarding the trouble I have pronouncing "woman" and "women." They sound exactly the same to me when I encode and decode it. But that's life, and there's no use getting upset about it.

Mary and Justin with a boy who is blind and deaf

Troy claims that I've never been angry at anyone. I'll admit that it's not in my nature to yell. I believe that my hearing loss has helped me learn to love all people, regardless of their mood. When you deal with the trials I had to face at a young age, someone else's bad mood is not a big deal. We all need someone to care about us in order to make it through life.

That's what families are for, and I feel there's nothing more important than good relationships with God and family.

Consider the scripture, "Love thy neighbor as thyself." (Matthew 5:43). I sincerely believe in that philosophy. It was shocking to see a news report that included a video clip of a man hit by a car. The image of him lying on the populated street with no one stopping to help was heartbreaking. I was astonished that any human being could walk past him as though he were a scrap of litter. It's tragic to think this is the kind of society a lot of people have become accustomed to.

Why aren't we helping people more? How can you see a car hit someone and just walk by? We can't let those things happen. We need to watch over and care about one another. When we care for each other, we are actually caring for ourselves, mending our own heart, and making the world a better place for all of us to live in.

"Look upon the bright side of life, to be cheerful, humble, prayerful."

– Hyrum Smith

Chapter **28**

Even as an adult, my love for sports has never left me. The positive team influence has stayed so strong in my heart that when I discovered the local Manti High School had approved soccer as a school sport in 2008, I immediately contacted the administration about helping coach the team. Ben Schoppe and I were given assistant coach positions under head coach Gerald Wayman.

I work hard at being positive with all the players and believe in giving solid, practical instruction on a level that they understand. I know from experience that positive reinforcement works best toward improving skills. Telling my boys what they do wrong is a necessary part of coaching, but telling them what they do right helps create a constructive environment that leaves them feeling like champions.

Gerald had an opportunity to observe first hand an advantage of my hearing loss. One of the games we played required a four-hour road trip, one way. In a bus full of teenage boys, I would just turn my hearing aids off, read a good book, do homework for school, or do e-mails via phone for my job. Gerald had no choice but to sit and listen—or do his best to ignore the noise.

When I first started coaching, some of the kids had to pay close attention to understand what I was saying because of the slight deaf accent in my speech. But as they spent more time around me, they grew accustomed to it.

I enjoy working with Gerald and the boys. Soccer runs in my blood. I even think about the team when I'm traveling the world for work. Part of my job is to gather donations from influential people who are in a position to make a difference. Sometimes I'll make an off-hand comment and update to coach Gerald like, "Hey, it was great to meet with Tony Romo and the rest of the Dallas Cowboys football team last week because they were generous enough to help raise enough money for a hearing aid mission in Africa!"

Justin in Africa

One time I had to miss our opening soccer match to meet with some NBA players. I sent a text message to Gerald asking how our team was doing. His return message stated, "We're winning so far. How's your meeting?" I replied that I was in the middle of a luncheon with Kevin Garnett, who wanted to know our soccer game score.

Perhaps the most exotic location I called Gerald from was Mount Everest, the tallest peak on the planet. It was a fitting place, since soccer always makes me feel like I'm on top of the world!

During the last week of our soccer season, I was in Africa distributing hearing aids. I didn't realize I would be smack in the middle of a dangerous safari camp scary enough to turn your hair ghostly white.

It began when we flew from the relative safety of Gaborone into the deep bush of Botswana. The wilderness surrounding the village of

Maun, Botswana, was full of wildlife and short on modern amenities. With no hotel in sight, we camped out under the baobab trees. The dark night was fast approaching when we returned from a two-hour jeep safari. It was exciting to see lions, elephants, rhinos, leopards, and hyenas as primitive as when they stepped off Noah's ark.

Justin with a baby rhino

My natural love for the outdoors extended to the African bush. I was thrilled to camp out in the wilderness amid the incredible sounds of African wildlife. As remarkable as the noises were, I was constantly on the alert for a lion's roar. I did not want to be on their menu. I crawled into my tent and climbed into my sleeping bag, hoping there were no snakes and bugs that had crept in while I was out.

I slept peacefully and awoke completely rested after what seemed like eight minutes, but was really eight hours. I jumped up, full of excitement for the upcoming morning game ride. Sipping some hot chocolate around the campfire, I noticed that everyone else appeared utterly exhausted.

"What's going on?" I asked.

"That was the scariest night of my life!" someone answered.

I listened in amazement to stories of the evening's personal encounters with wildlife. Elephants, hyenas, and lions had invaded the camp, growling and howling all around our tents. Bill had responded to a hyena's growling laughter with an eerie laugh of his own, which only seemed to aggravate the beast. Come to think of it, Bill's hair appeared a shade whiter than the night before. Several members of our party were terrified. Others saw it as a grand adventure.

I was extremely disappointed to find out that I had missed a roundup and party of wild African animals right outside my tent. I had slept through the whole stampede. Again, hearing loss can be a blessing or a curse. But one thing I learned from this experience was that I was never going to step out of my tent in the middle of the night to water a tree, in case lions might see me as a main course entrée.

Since I survived the safari, I was able to send Gerald pictures of little African kids who'd just been fitted with hearing aids. Gerald said it was nice to be able to share the photos with the team to let them know what I was doing and why I couldn't be with them. When I was home and available to make team practice, I would try to teach my boys that service can be found no matter where you are, and not just in Africa.

I'm honored to serve with Coach Wayman and grateful for the opportunity to be on this soccer team. Sometimes my boys call me for an impromptu game of soccer, just for the fun of it. If I'm in town and available, I'm more than willing to show them my fancy footwork. But they still kick my butt. Whatever the score, I just love, love, love to play soccer!

Justin in Africa

"Never measure your life by the days you have lived, but by the smiles you leave behind."

— *William, from Mexico*

Chapter 29

Without hearing aids, people who are deaf can only see what they can't hear: people's mouths move with no sound, silent cars roll past, quiet birds swoop through the sky. But the gift of hearing offers the listener the ability to hear what he sees, to participate in the joy of laughter, to connect with other people through sharing feelings, and the freedom to move about without worry of unheard danger.

I recognize all the wonderful people throughout my life who have helped me. Without the tedious repetition of speech and listening therapy, the patient guidance through schoolwork, and all the emotional support and encouragement, I would not have grown to become who I am today. Even though I didn't thank all those people who changed my life at the time, I wish to thank them now.

When I turned twenty-nine, I had a strong desire to find my first speech pathologist, Carol Keltsch. I wanted to thank her for never giving up on me, because I was a scrappy little kid. Some would even call me a scoundrel. I'd left Carol's tutelage before I learned how to speak very well. I thought it would be fun to go back and tell her, "Thanks to you, I can hear with conviction and speak with passion."

Mother drove with me back to Carol's neighborhood. We had no idea if she was even still alive, let alone if she lived in the same house where she taught speech therapy in her basement. The passing landscape only brought vague memories to my mind, but as soon as Mother drove up to the house, I felt like I was three years old all over again.

Mother parked, and we got out. At first I was puzzled as we moved up the front walk because everything seemed out of proportion. It was all so small. I reached out and knocked on a door that wasn't as tall as it used to be. Mother and I waited until, at last, the door opened and Carol Keltsch herself looked up at me from a wheelchair. I had no doubt it was her, even though she had silver linings in her hair and her face was softly wrinkled. Her eyes were still kind and patient when she asked, "How may I help you?" She obviously didn't recognize me.

In a sudden wash of memories, I realized how much time she had spent patiently teaching me how to make sounds. I remembered her smile whether I got it right or not. Her unfailing good nature had made a big difference in my progress toward speech. She made it fun, and she made me believe I could do it. The bubbles we blew were a crucial step toward my higher education—a priceless gift.

I gave my first speech teacher a tender smile. "You've already helped me."

Her eyes went wide, and I saw recognition light up their depths. Her chin quivered as she whispered, "Justin?"

"Yes," I answered. "I'm the three-year-old Justin Osmond you taught." I leaned forward and took her soft hand in mine. "I want to thank you for never giving up on me."

Her smile could have lit up Manhattan. She invited us in, where we sat and talked and laughed about the good old times. She shared what had gone on in her life since then; I told her all about what I was doing; Mother shared her experiences, and we had a wonderful reunion.

For all you speech therapists out there, and to the mothers and fathers of children having challenges learning to speak and hear, don't ever give up on them. All the hard work will pay off. I can't thank selfless people like Carol, Nancy, and Bill enough for helping me make my dreams come true.

The development that takes place during childhood tends to affect us the most later in life. I truly enjoy helping anyone—regardless of age—receive the gift of better hearing. But if we don't take care of the future, the future won't take care of itself. Children are our future leaders, and it's our responsibility to care for them with food, shelter, love—and hearing aids, if needed.

Justin counseling and training a child on how
to take care of a hearing aid

Justin loves being with children, including those
who are hearing impaired

The best situation is not needing hearing aids at all. Because I know what deafness is like, I've become an ambassador to support various hearing conservation programs, such as Starkey's "Sound Matters" hearing initiative. Each of us is responsible to conserve our hearing to the best of our ability. In spite of the fact that I've pointed out occasional benefits of deafness, I'm glad that I'm able to hear when I need to. The thought of remaining deaf, with no chance of hearing, is sobering, to say the least. If I had to pick one sense to keep, I'd pick hearing, because the value of being able to hear is priceless. Don't take it for granted.

In today's fast-paced, noisy society, we often forget to listen. The loud music, ipods, traffic, and media all around us occupy our physical senses on a daily basis. It's nice to be able to hear all these sounds, but they can be a distraction. One of the reasons there is a steadily increasing demand for hearing aids is the tendency for ipod listeners to crank up the volume. As a result, their hearing days are numbered. It's tragic that one in five American teenagers now suffers from some type of hearing loss, an increase of 31% since the mid 90s. [10]

I caution every ipod user not to blast your eardrums. It's just not cool to crank things up because you can—especially if it's so loud you damage your ears for the remainder of your life. Go ahead and enjoy the music, but preserve your hearing now so you can have it for a lifetime. I promise that when you get older, you'll be grateful you did. You'll be watching all those other people go in search of audiologists for hearing aids so they can hear their grandchildren's sweet voices.

The traditional joke is that older people tune in to classical music while younger music-lovers choose rock and roll. I'll admit to enjoying classical music, and I'm not old! Without my hearing aids, I have approximately a 10% hearing discrimination, which means I can grasp one out of ten words correctly. With hearing aids, the discrimination goes up to around 75%. Basically, I can't pick out all the words in a song, so occasionally I prefer classical music without words. Music just makes life better, as long as it's flowing into the ear canal instead of blasting through it.

The Early Hearing Detection and Intervention program (EHDI) states that hearing loss occurs in approximately 12,000 newborn children each year (up to 3 of every 1,000 births). According to the National Institute on Deafness and Other Communication Disorders

(NIDCD), about 28 million people in the U.S. have some degree of reduced hearing. An estimated 15% of children and teenagers in the United States have a temporary or permanent hearing loss in one or both ears. [11]

The National Institute on Deafness and Other Communication Disorders states that, "Hearing impairment is a growing public health concern. An estimated 28 million Americans suffer from some type of hearing loss, and 500,000 to 750,000 Americans have severe to profound hearing impairment or deafness. Furthermore, more people are losing their hearing earlier in life. As people live longer, and the survival rate for medically fragile infants improves, the number of people with hearing loss will undoubtedly increase.

"Although more and more Americans are experiencing a gradual reduction in hearing as they age, in 1999–2000, only 29 percent of adults ages 20 to 69 had their hearing tested. As for hearing aids, only approximately 15 percent of hearing-impaired adults ages 20-69 use one. Data from 2001 indicate 150 of every 1,000 adults with hearing loss use a hearing aid." [12]

A lot of people are ashamed and don't want others to know they have a hearing loss. But if they'd stop and think about it, they'd soon realize that the hearing loss is more obvious than a hearing aid.

If you're still around in 2025, I predict that you'll see more people wearing hearing aids because they didn't use hearing protection. In almost all cases, simple precautions can prevent hearing loss. I urge people to turn down the music and wear hearing protection if they're working with noisy equipment. I really hate to think of anyone suffering later, wishing they'd taken better care of their hearing when they could have. I couldn't control my hearing loss; I urge you not to needlessly go through the same thing I've had to endure.

"Between the great things that we can't do and the small things we will not do lies the danger that we will not do anything at all."

– Adolph Monod

Chapter 30

I was once the keynote speaker in the Dallas Cowboys football Stadium for hundreds of Texas teens who were hearing-impaired. At that time, if a Texas student's best-hearing ear had a decibel (DB) loss of 70 or more, he or she could be awarded a full college scholarship. The problem was, these kids weren't taking advantage of this incredible opportunity. My goal was to motivate them to go to college and get an education so they could work at a career they enjoyed.

Unfortunately, self-esteem within the deaf culture is usually not very high. It is convenient to use hearing loss as an excuse not to do something that is out of the comfort zone, such as going to college. In an effort to help them overcome their fears of inadequacy, I said, "You have a college scholarship opportunity for which, if given the chance, I would have become a Texas citizen, just so I could take advantage of it. A hearing loss is no excuse to limit yourself." I encouraged them to at least give it a try. After all, nothing ventured, nothing gained.

I hope my words made a difference in the way they saw this opportunity, because I firmly believe that no one gains anything if they don't go for it. We have two ends in life—one to think with and one to sit on. The one we use most will determine how well we do in life. In other words, heads you win, tails you lose.

My early childhood development of hard-work ethics paid off as I learned to get off my tail end and be as productive as possible. I'm grateful for the opportunities to travel to many countries around the world such as India, Egypt, Malawi, Mozambique, Botswana, Zambia, Zimbabwe, Kenya, Venezuela, Vietnam, Peru, Guatemala, Nicaragua, and many others. The life stories I encounter on my travels are poignant, life changing, and true. Again, I must reiterate my sincere thanks to all those who have contributed and continue to make it possible so that many of our hearing impaired brothers and sisters will have a chance at tomorrow. Like Bill Austin says, "We can't do much alone, but together we can change the world."

In Guadalajara, Mexico, a slender forty-year-old lady tripped on the doorjamb of our clinic just as she entered. Her attentive husband caught her before she fell, then explained in Spanish, "I'm sorry, she cannot see well, and she cannot hear." He stood as close to her as permitted during the fitting process. Eyes squinted, she turned her head toward him, and he reached in to touch her hand. Her fingers curled around his and held on. Finally her hearing aids were in. She burst into tears and clapped her hands to her face. Her husband wrapped his arms around her. "Te amo," he said, stroking her hair in a way that calmed her. Safe in her husband's familiar arms, she lowered her hands and squinted around the room, tears still falling, her face an incredulous smile of joy combined with nervous anticipation at the bombardment of unfamiliar noises. Forty soundless years are hard to ignore. Mature brains settle into patterns that formed at a young age, and they don't like changing. Adult speech and listening therapy is much more difficult and less effective than therapy for children. In this case, the younger the better, but it's never too late. That forty-year-old woman was able to hear her husband say, "I love you" for the first time in her life. That is beyond imagination.

A little boy in Mexico City was so excited when he heard his first sound that he actually jumped up and started dancing. He thought he was so cool, and we agreed. Captivated by his outgoing personality, we decided to follow him home to see how he'd respond to household sounds. Watching him flinch and stare at his dog demonstrated that he had never heard his pet bark before. When he got a drink of water, he gasped and stuck his fingers in the clear running water, then turned the faucet off and on and off and on to listen to the running water splash into the sink. He could scarcely believe the sound coming out of the television, and examined it front and back, placing his ear close to the warm speaker. The best part was still to come. I was amused to see that when he discovered the sound of the toilet flushing, he stood beside it, pushing the handle over and over to marvel at the growling gargle of water spiraling down the hole.

In El Salvador, we met a mother who brought her two little girls into the clinic without an appointment. We got to work, fitting both sisters with hearing aids. The mother sat quietly against the wall, hands clasped in her lap, eyes following every move we made as though her life depended on it. We didn't learn the whole story until after the girls—shiny eyed with wonder at their new world of sound— disappeared down the road with their grateful mother. In order to bring her girls to our hearing mission site, this woman had sold her only source of income—a milk cow. We also discovered it would take them two days of walking to finally reach their home.

I stared at the empty road where I'd last seen the mother carefully shepherding her precious girls, one on each side. I wondered if there was any way to find her. I wanted to know what she would do for her livelihood now. How would she continue to feed and clothe her daughters? It was sobering to think of all she had given up in order to

Justin with sisters who needed hearing aids

help her girls. Her actions reminded me of my own mother's sacrifices. It is amazing to see the incredible things mothers do for their children. My mother is my hero, because—like that mother in El Salvador—my mother would have walked two days on foot if that's what it took to help me hear. Mothers who never give up are the greatest asset children have.

Once we learned this woman's story, we desperately wanted to help her. Because she was a walk-in, we didn't have her contact information, so it seemed hopeless.

Six months later, we received a simple letter from the mother of these two girls. She painstakingly wrote about how much better they were doing in school and how grateful she was that they could hear. She ended with the simple words, "Thank you, thank you, thank you so much for making their dreams come true." Fortunately for us, the letter had a return address.

Bill Austin is a very generous man who took the necessary steps to purchase a milk cow, then had it delivered to this mother. I'm sure this lady was not expecting any blessing above having her girls hear, but now her livelihood was suddenly restored. I wish I could have been there to see her face when the cow was led into her yard and the rope passed over into her hand.

Every time I see a little girl or boy hear for their first time, I can only imagine what it was like when I first heard my mother's voice. Because I was so young, I have a hard time remembering the first time I heard anything. But every time I see these kids light up, I can't help but speculate what it must have been like for me. Hearing your loved ones reconnects family and brings a feeling of joy that you can't get anywhere else.

A girl in Cuzco, Peru, lived for ten years without sound. Then a couple of little devices in her ears awakened her to a world full of noises of such variety that she wasn't sure where to look to find what was making the sound. Her parents, grandparents, and all her siblings stood around her, crying tears of joy. Their love for this little girl was evident.

Then her mother came up to me. Wiping her eyes, she said, "I'm so grateful. I never thought my daughter would be able to hear. I didn't realize all the opportunities she was missing. Now she can communicate, get an education, and a good job." Her next words totally blew me away. "Out of love for my daughter, I wondered if there's any way that you would adopt her and take her back to America so she could have even greater opportunities."

I was momentarily speechless. I had never imagined that anyone would ever offer me their own child. It was flattering to be trusted enough that they would ask me to take her, but I encouraged the mother to keep her daughter with the family, to love her, encourage her, and help her succeed.

Another family in Vietnam brought in a young boy who was struggling in elementary school because he couldn't hear the teacher. Actually, he was failing miserably. His worried parents couldn't afford the hearing aids he needed, so the Starkey Hearing Foundation fitted this fine young man.

We did follow-ups with him every year after that. Our observations showed that after barely passing elementary school, he did better in middle school, and ultimately finished high school as the valedictorian. All these good things happened in his life because someone gave him a chance to hear.

Justin with young man happy to hear

A young girl in Mexico, living in the poorest of circumstances, had no chance of getting help until we came along. Seeing her experience sound for the first time in her life was the best feeling in the world. William, the father of this beautiful little girl, came up to me afterward to express incredible gratitude that his little daughter could now hear and take advantage of the opportunities that lay before her. He spoke humble words that I will never forget. "It is like a beacon of light has come into my family." Then he twisted his hat in his hands for a moment, swallowing back tears. His daughter laughed, and he turned his head to watch her throw her arms around her mother.

At last he turned around and spoke words I will never, ever forget. With all the sincerity in his heart, William said, "I hope you never measure your life by the days you've lived, but by the smiles you've left behind. Thank you for bringing this beautiful smile to my daughter's face.

Although I don't take personal credit for his daughter's hearing, this humble man's words took me by surprise. The more I thought about them, the more they rang true. Striving to live an extended life for the sake of breathing for more days than anyone else on the planet is not the most important thing. What good is reaching the hundred-year mark if all those years are filled with selfishness and regret? Better, if you must, to have fewer years filled with joy and love, giving and helping as much as your heart can hold. Things are not as important as people. I've never seen a man drive his Cadillac to Heaven. To leave smiles behind when you go, is the greatest legacy you could wish for. I have taken this wise man's words and engraved them into my heart.

Justin with smiling girl
"Life is measured by the smiles you leave behind."

"Don't ever give up on your dream. There are thousands of souls depending on those dreams."

— Olive Osmond

Chapter **31**

On January 23, 2003, I visited my Osmond grandparents in their home in Ephraim, Utah. They greeted me warmly, and I settled down to have a heartfelt talk with them. The conversation turned serious, and the words my grandmother Olive spoke stirred my soul like never before. I didn't know it was to be my last visit before my grandmother died. I did take the time to write down some of her thoughts/ feelings/words.

Olive Osmond had a dream to one day have a foundation that would donate all their time and resources to help the deaf. Her sons Virl and Tom have sacrificed many things in this life without the gift of hearing. She mentioned that with my distinctive hearing loss, I would be able to help, assist and lead the way to provide many men, women, and children with better hearing due to the advanced technology available and the generosity of many. I remember hearing my grandparents discuss for hours how in a coming day her beloved sons–as well as the deaf community–would be blessed. She stressed the importance of staying dedicated to the task and focus on leading the work that the original dream of the Osmond Foundation was set up to do. Then I remember her words, "Don't ever give up on your dream. There are thousands of souls depending on those dreams."

This powerful message infused me with the momentum to be able to do all that I'm doing today. The matriarch of the famous singing Osmonds, known world-wide by the affectionate nickname, "Mother Osmond," made a life-long commitment to support new research toward improving the quality of life for the hearing impaired. Her efforts were motivated by her two oldest sons who are severely hearing impaired, which led to the establishment of the Osmond Foundation—an organization intended to promote hearing health awareness. Over time, the Osmond Foundation grew into the Children's Miracle Network, a very worthy cause that expanded far beyond what Mother Osmond began.

I felt very close to my grandmother and loved hearing the stories she told about helping other children who were deaf. Her experiences inspired me. I also know that she and Bill Austin had conversed a couple of times over the phone, sharing their similar dreams, visions, and aspirations in serving the needs of the hearing impaired. Knowing that Grandmother was so intent on doing everything she could to make the world more accessible to me and others with hearing loss made her an absolute hero in my eyes.

Sensing her determination to serve the hearing impaired, I dedicated myself to continue her passion in building her dream to greater heights. Motivated by the unconditional love I shared with my grandmother, I established the Olive Osmond Perpetual Hearing Fund, reinstating my grandmother's original purpose for the Osmond Foundation. It is very rewarding to be a part of re-establishing Mother Osmond's original dream of raising deaf awareness and promoting hearing educational services by providing others with the gift of better hearing. Everyone can share in the joy of giving by becoming "Hearing Angels"—the name given to those who help with funds raised to sponsor hearing humanitarian missions.

The unselfish dedication of Hearing Angels will allow children to hear the wondrous sounds of the world around them. When you see the delight that people experience when they first hear the sounds we take for granted every day, it makes you stop and think. Perhaps you'll tilt your head and listen more closely to birds tweeting, the whisper of leaves in the wind, and the sound of joyous laughter, which can suddenly fill your heart to brimming over with gratitude for the gift of sound.

In the words of Thomas S. Monson, "We build our income by what we get, but we build our lives by what we give." Let's continue to build lives by providing hope to all those we meet with small acts of kindness. Even a smile can make someone's day infinitely better. And if we are able, let's help provide the miracle of hearing to those who would never have the opportunity to receive it without our help. Many people around the world may have a hearing loss, but with the generosity of those I like to call "HEAR-O's," their hearing loss will no longer have them.

I invite you to visit *www.OliveOsmond.com*, a site that explains our mission, our motivation, and the different ways you can help. As we align with the Starkey Hearing Foundation and welcome sponsorship opportunities, we will be able to help thousands of children worldwide in honor of the unselfish legacy Olive Osmond left behind.

"Whether you think you can or think you can't, you're right."
– Henry Ford

Chapter 32

After watching me struggle with my hearing loss, Shane feels that he can accomplish anything he puts his mind to. He still can't quite grasp the fact that I count my hearing loss as one of my greatest blessings. But that's truly the way I see it. Most people look at a miracle as something God has done that we have no control over. I see my abilities as miracles created by God and implemented with hard work.

While Shane and I studied for our MBA (Master of Business Administration) degrees, he mentioned that he sometimes wished for a set of hearing aids he could turn off to achieve complete focus. Who wouldn't want to study in peace and quiet?

Another benefit to the hardships in my life is that they've made me very goal oriented. The other side of the coin would be to give up—but that's never going to happen!

Recently, I set a goal to run a marathon. This was a giant step from running two-mile track events or the length of a soccer field during a game. Due to my busy schedule, I have limited time to run. In order to fit in more training, I set up an early morning running time with some close friends. Only very good friends would be crazy enough to wake each other up at four in the morning. Otherwise, a person might get a slipper smacked right between the eyes. So, while sane people sleep in their warm beds, we're out in our running shoes with the cold nipping our legs and barely enough light to see the road. One good thing about running at that time is that there's no traffic, no exhaust fumes, and no need to dodge pedestrians. We have the world to ourselves. The air is crisp and clear with an explosion of stars overhead.

On long 10-15 mile runs, I don't usually wear my hearing aids. My buddies talk among themselves, and I can't hear them. Despite being left out of their conversation, they still accept me just how I am. We've even developed our own form of communication where they'll tap my shoulder and give me a thumbs up to ask how I'm doing. If I'm fine, I return the thumbs up. I appreciate their thoughtfulness. When they return to conversing among themselves, I run along with them under the starry canopy of the heavens, enjoying long talks with my best friend, Heavenly Father. Sometimes I even throw in a prayer that I can make it to the end!

Justin's first marathon

My lifetime goal is to compete in a triathlon. Because of my intense training regime, I recently came home from a tough workout consisting of bicycling, swimming, and running. I was beat. I knew if I lay down for even a moment to rest, I'd fall asleep. So I made myself get in the shower first. I ran it hot enough to help relax my aching muscles, soaking up the spray of steaming water until the water heater emptied. Then I put on my bathrobe, wiped the mist off the mirror, and started brushing my teeth.

All of a sudden I became aware of frantic pounding on the door. Startled, I opened it to see my parents' frightened faces. "What's going on?" I asked.

"Can't you hear the fire alarm?" Mother asked with wide, anxious eyes.

"No."

"What happened to make it go off?" Father asked.

I didn't know any more than they did. They told me that when they came over to visit me, the house fire alarm was going ballistic. My parents ran all over the place trying to figure out if there was any real danger. When everything looked safe, they tried to find out how to turn off the alarm.

I was just brushing my teeth with no clue.

I'm cautious, but honestly, I don't know what set off the alarm. I don't see how the shower could have done it, but whatever it was, I know I'll have to deal with things like that for the rest of my life.

In spite of these occasional reminders of my limitations, I feel very blessed. I want to help other people believe in themselves so they, in turn, can encourage others to follow their dreams. Who would have ever thought this profoundly deaf toddler could ever play the violin/viola, let alone earn a music Sterling Scholarship, play piano, drums, and sing on stage with my father?

You're the only one who can do something about the kind of person you want to become. Think about what you've been given in life and what you do with it. Will you dare try something you've always wanted to do? Will you put yourself out to speak to someone new? Or are you going to sit in a corner and watch everyone else live their lives to the fullest? It's up to you. A Sanscrit maxim says, "For yesterday is but a dream and tomorrow is only a vision but today well lived makes every yesterday a dream of happiness and every tomorrow a vision of hope."

Please don't tell people they're not good enough. Even if they're amateurs, let them experience joy and failures that help build toward their future success. The only way to get better at something is to keep working at it. Encouragement is just as easy to give as discouragement, but it makes everyone feel a whole lot better.

Sometimes nice surprises come along when you follow your passion. During a family vacation to Wales a couple of years ago, the Wales Archery Team put on a traditional long bow shooting demonstration for us. Afterwards, they asked if we would like a turn to shoot at the targets. My brothers and I were used to modern compound bows, but were willing to give their longbows a try. I turned off my hearing aids, accepted a bow and arrow from a burly team member, focused, took aim, and hit the bull's eye. The guy who'd handed me the bow stared at the target, then at me, then back at the target. "Are you kidding me?" he asked.

I was perfectly serious.

An enthusiastic invitation to join their team followed. There was an important competition coming up the next month, and they really wanted me in their ranks. But I was going to be back in the United States, so I had to decline.

I sincerely hope that no one ever feels they have to limit themselves. With faith, hard work, and according to God's will, anything can happen.

I've learned that one of the best ways to overcome challenges is to have a strong and personal relationship with our Savior, Jesus Christ. He knows all pain. He cares deeply about us, even as we suffer. If none of us had any disabilities, we wouldn't grow stronger. Without weaknesses, we tend to ignore or disregard our Savior. No wonder He says that He gives us weaknesses that we may be humble. He also offers to help us turn our weaknesses into strengths. The secret in life is to let our weaknesses take us to a higher level. It's so comforting to realize that God knows everything about us and still loves us enough to give us what we need to turn those weaknesses into our greatest blessings. We are all beggars who rely completely on our Savior for each breath we take. Once we understand the true purposes of God and his plan, then we realize that those who best can suffer, can best endure.

Orson Whitney said, "No pain that we suffer, no trial that we experience is wasted. It ministers to our education, to the development of such qualities as patience, faith, fortitude, and humility. All that we suffer and all that we endure, especially when we endure it patiently, builds up our characters, purifies our hearts, expands our souls and makes us more tender and charitable. And it is through sorrow and suffering, toil and tribulation that we gain the education that we come here to acquire."

Because my hearing loss gave me a disadvantage compared to those around me, I became tenaciously determined. Somewhere along the way, I believed that I could do anything I set my mind to. In other words, if it's to be, it's up to me. I've proven this concept over and over again. Working harder than anyone else on the playing field meant I didn't necessarily keep my starting position out of talent, but from sheer determination.

Despite our best intentions, our spiritual enemy can take any good thing and twist it to the dark side. My determination could subtly switch to an attempt to impose my will upon the Lord. This is where I learned the very difficult lesson: no matter how determined I was or how hard I worked, I could not force my will upon the Lord. I had to stop, admit defeat, and hand my life over, saying, "Not my will, but Thine be done."

This is not to say that people shouldn't be determined. I know I can do hard things—we can all do hard things. As Garth Brooks says, "There's bound to be rough waters, and I know I'll take some falls, but with the good Lord as my captain, I can make it through them all." Simply change your paradigm thinking. Do everything you can to reach your goals, then be willing to let God ultimately guide your path, even if you can't see where He's leading you. We're truly like blind men feeling our way through the darkness, doing the best we know how. We'd do much better if we remember that Heavenly Father is the light that shines in the darkness; we'd be wise to follow Him.

I'm so determined to qualify for the Boston Marathon that I'm going to keep on running. But if for any reason God has other plans and ultimately pulls the pavement out from under me, then I'm willing to accept that. Now, if it's to be, it's up to me and the will of Heavenly Father.

My father says, "Where there is humility, the Lord's spirit abides. Where there is compassion, the depth of love is found. Where there is repentance, the mercy of Christ is given. Where there is sacrifice, the blessings of heaven await. Where there is faith, the miracles are bestowed. Where there is pain, a test is given for sure. Where much is given, much more is required. Where much is lost, much more will be gained."

So let there be joy in life's journey—including your adversity! I'm here to tell you it can be done. Find the good portion of any problem. View trials as stepping stones to build a better, happier, stronger, funnier, and more resilient self. Become the kind of person you're really meant to be, and you'll be much happier.

I promise.

"The obstacles before you are never as strong as the power within you."

— Anonymous

Chapter 33

There is a problem with placing yourself in a "poor me" scenario. I'll admit there were times when I believed I deserved extra attention, pity, and special accommodations because I was deaf. I have yet to find an instance when having such an attitude ever did me any good.

I'd like to share a four-step formula I've used along the way that has helped me accept what can't be changed, or if it can be changed, what to do about it. Anyone can use this formula and apply it to their own lives.

1. Recognize your challenges.

How do you overcome them if you don't know what they are? For example, I came home one day with brand new hearing aids. When Shane noticed them, he pointed and asked, "What kind is it?"

I said, "It's about 5:30 p.m."

I recognized that I had a problem. Troubles are easier to deal with if you view them with humor. In my case, unlike Uncle Donny and Aunt Marie on "Dancing With the Stars," I keep on dancing when the music stops . . . but I also keep on smiling.

Donny, Justin, and Marie Osmond

2. Accept your challenges.

Once you acknowledge what your challenge is, the second step is to accept it. What you have is part of who you are, not what you are. Who you are is your true self. Have you noticed that you are a lot happier when you accept yourself? Challenges that pass through us, like my deafness, are inevitable. But how we pass through the challenges is completely under our own control.

When I met a good friend in Colombia, I took him out for a steak dinner. As we were eating, I asked, "Isn't this the best steak you've ever had?"

He answered, "This is the same steak I've always had."

I didn't understand what he meant by that. Surely he knew that South American beef is legendary for its quality. How could he not notice a difference?

He must have read the confusion on my face, for he said, "Justin, you didn't know this before, but I have no sense of taste. But I'm not going to let that get in the way of enjoying my dinner."

His positive attitude hit me right in the heart. He had every right to be bitter about not tasting his food or drink, but he chose to be better. That's been a great learning model for me. You may as well accept challenges, because if there's nothing you can do about them, why worry? How much complaining will make them go away? Since the answer is obviously "none," why dwell on it? Accept it, live with it, and don't let it get in the way of enjoying life.

Some people compare themselves to others, thinking, "If only I were like so-and-so with their job/house/looks/life, all my problems would be gone." Trying to imitate someone else will never duplicate them. Please don't become the victim of another's agenda. Being honest with yourself is the only way to truly feel good. A good attitude will turn hard times into valuable lessons.

Imagine the lesson learned by my friend who took off one early spring day to hike in the mountains. As he reveled in the tender beauty of new flowers pushing through the dark earth and bright green leaves dressing the tree limbs, he felt connected with nature. A little farther on, he realized he'd wandered a little too close to nature when a rattlesnake suddenly struck, sending its poisonous fangs burning into his tender flesh.

Why? My friend hadn't done anything wrong. It was just something that unexpectedly happened.

Now he had two choices. He could become bitter, shouting out his anger and wishing to kick the tar out of the snake for inflicting undeserved pain. But if he had ranted and raved, the venom would have pervaded his system, slowly destroying him while he screamed about the unfairness of it all.

His other choice was to take a deep breath, suck the venom out, if possible, and go for help to get every drop of poison out of his system.

It's a universal truth that unfortunate things happen in life. It's what we do with what happens that makes the difference. Compare a snake's venom to hatred. We could let hatred build up within, making us so bitter that it eventually kills our souls. Or we could stop, look at the situation, learn a lesson, and say, "I'm just going to release the hatred, accept the outcome, and simply move on without a backward glance."

No one I know escapes life without problems. Most of us have them heaped on us, whether we like it or not. It's part of life. It's up to us how we look at it. My father taught me that if there's nothing you can do about it, why worry about it? You can either laugh or cry, but if you laugh, people will like you more.

Accept any challenge as an opportunity, not a penalty. It's not a curse but a blessing, not a demotion but a promotion. Throw out the idea that it's an impairment, because it's an advantage. Reject embarrassment and turn it around to become an honor and privilege. It's no accident, it's a contribution to life. You do not have a handicap, it's a miracle. All the challenges I've gone through are so small compared to the strength they've given me. Like a squirming caterpillar transforming into an iridescent butterfly, you can turn any challenge into a beautiful, positive thing.

My lack of hearing does not bring me down. It's only my own lack of hope, commitment, faith, or courage that hurt me. My own fear of not being accepted for who I am brings misery on myself. It was a hard lesson for me to learn that once you accept yourself for who you are, others will accept you, too. One of the mysteries of life is that if I can truly understand with my heart, then my challenges become lightened, and I can feel God's guidance and direction in my life.

The same is true for you. One of God's greatest miracles is to enable ordinary people to do extraordinary things.

3. Overcome fear, inadequacies, and consequences.

I love every member of my family, but my true heroes are my parents. They taught me that I can overcome anything that stands in my way. My father taught me over and over again that if I fear failure, I do not have the faith sufficient enough to believe that God will lead me to my final destiny.

I love socializing with close friends and making new friends everywhere I go. However, like in many social gathering where everyone is talking in a jumble of words flying about the room, my brain tends to struggle with the overall atmosphere of collecting data and footage all around me. At times like that, it's very difficult for me. What is the group topic of conversation? Aside from all the noise in the room, my hearing aid microphone tries to pick up what's really being said and who is saying what.

Many times I'll resort to just sitting quietly, watching with my eagle eyes to try and put the different social pieces of the puzzle together. This build-up of mental exertion often leads to complete exhaustion. If this group event takes place in a dining atmosphere, I'll sometimes just eat my meal in isolated silence because there's nothing for me to say—especially when I have no idea what the group topic is about.

Then all of a sudden the room will become completely quiet and I will look up to see everyone staring at me expecting some form of a direct response. Just imagine yourself in my shoes at that moment. What do you say to save yourself from embarrassment? It's not that I wasn't paying attention and coming across as rude. It's simply because I was unable to follow the primary conversation at hand.

The next thing I know, the room would be filled with loud laughter and ridicule. In all honesty, these little acts of misunderstanding make it extremely uncomfortable for someone like me, who wants nothing more than to simply be united and on the same page as everyone else.

That's not to say that I am anti-social. Quite the opposite. Anyone who understands my heart knows that I love people very much. This lack of hearing can lead to a lack of social interaction, which can then directly affect my emotional, physical, and intellectual well-being. Despite all of this, I press forward with a cheerful heart, knowing that I can always find joy in whatever journey I may be in.

While I was in college, my friend invited me to his house for a dinner party. As we assembled at the table, a lady I'd never met before sat down at my right. It didn't take me long to realize that this young woman had no arms or hands. My first thought was, "How is she going to eat?" I'm sure that others wondered the same thing. I wasn't sure how to respond to this situation. But I'm very sensitive to other people's challenges, and I wanted to be sure she got to eat, too. I was more than willing to help her. So, after we bowed our heads and blessed our food, I turned to ask if she needed help. Before I could say a word, I witnessed something I'll never forget. Scarcely believing her ingenuity, I watched as both of her clean, bare feet came up to the table. With the agility of a graceful daddy longleg spider, she grabbed a utensil with the toes of each foot and slowly, yet steadily, picked up her food and ate it. It was very impressive— beyond anything I'd ever seen.

I guarantee that everyone in that room was humbled and

suddenly grateful for their fingers. Most people don't give a second thought to how they eat. They simply use their hands, paying more attention to how the food tastes than how it gets in their mouths. Yet here was a remarkable young lady with no hands or arms who could have easily come up with an excuse for not feeding herself. Who would have blamed her? Certainly not me. Yet she came up with a solution that was breathtaking. This incident gave me added inspiration in overcoming my own personal challenges. If she could do it, so could I.

And so can you.

I face a much smaller eating problem. I tend to chew with my mouth open. It's driven my family crazy over the years. One night when we were teenagers, Travis actually rigged a poster that read "Chew with your mouth shut" on the ceiling above the kitchen table so skillfully that I didn't even notice it. During the meal, Travis pulled a string, and the sign fell down in front of my face. It startled me enough that I remembered to focus on good table manners for the rest of that meal. But, unfortunately, it didn't cure me for good.

This habit of mine was especially distressing for my father because he's a professional. I don't intend to be impolite. The reason I chew so loudly and with my mouth open is because I can't hear myself chewing—whether it's gum or food. Another reason is that my whole speech and listening therapy education has been about how I place my tongue and mouth so the words would come out right. Words can't come out through closed lips, so I'm not very good at working my mouth and leaving my lips closed. This simply wasn't the way I was trained as a child, so it has an effect on how I eat.

A few decades ago, doctors and nurses didn't have the benefit of today's medicine, but did the best they could for wounded soldiers. The pain of suffering with lost arms, legs, or eyes was incredible. Emotional pain was as much a factor as physical distress. Even when their injuries were not life threatening, some patients simply gave up and died.

In an effort to bring hope to the wounded, the hospital staff hosted a guest speaker, praying that he would be able to lift the spirits of these soldiers and let them know they had fought for a good cause and there was hope for their future. When a well-dressed visitor arrived, he stood on a balcony overlooking the hospital floor. Gripping the railing with one hand, he leaned over and said in a booming voice, "I know what you guys are going through."

The wounded looked up at him standing over them on both legs in his fine clothes and began booing. You could almost read their thoughts. *You have no idea what we're going through. We're bleeding, in pain, and could die at any time. How can you feel empathy for us when you're not in pain as we are?*

When the room finally quieted, the speaker insisted in a quieter voice, "I know exactly what you're going through."

They booed him again, more viciously this time, with catcalls and jeers. Amidst the noise, the speaker walked to the head of a spiral staircase that led down to the wounded soldiers' floor. As he started down the steps, he fumbled with his shoulder, then gave an odd shake of his arm. As soon as he made the first spiral turn, he pulled his arm free of its sleeve and dropped it on the stairs.

The booing quit as suddenly as if it had been cut off with a hatchet. On the next turn, the speaker paused and bent over. After a few moments of fumbling, he pulled off one of his legs and dropped it on the stairs. Gripping the stair rail, he hopped down to the floor amid absolute silence. Then he reached down with his single remaining arm and removed his other leg. He had everyone's undivided attention as he sat his stump of a body on the bottom step.

"You don't think I know what you're going through, but I do," he said. "I'm living with only a partial body, yet I'm out there living my dreams as the CEO of a successful company. I'm president of my own thriving business because I'm not letting this"—he gestured to his legless body—"get in the way of me accomplishing all I want to do in life, and you shouldn't, either."

Another way of overcoming fear is to find the silver lining in the situation. Yes, there is always another side. Look until you find the advantages. In my case, it's being able to turn my hearing aids off. When I had to make the critical field goal in football, I turned off the distracting noise.

When I take a test in school, I turn my hearing aids off. For penalty kicks in soccer, it's just the goalie and me, even though people are screaming on all sides.

4. Share your story.

Don't be afraid to share your story, including your trials, challenges, and lessons you've learned. A dear friend taught me a powerful and valuable lesson which I try to apply in my daily life. It is that God has given us different means and senses to learn, grow and help us find our way home. Some examples are tools, vehicles, and maps, etc.; they are hearing, sight, taste, touch, and smell. He has also given us higher-powered senses that can be used in a powerful/meaningful way when our heart is pure. These greater senses are imagination, inspiration, will, reason, intuition, memory, and reception. So as we strive to listen with a pure heart, we are utilizing all of our resources to gain greater knowledge and understanding. The world teaches that our feelings are not valid and that the heart is not reliable, but the divine truth is that following our heart is the only way to get home.

You never know when something you say or do might help buoy someone up. For my Eagle Scout project, I wanted to share the precious gift of hearing. From that moment on, I've gone worldwide to help others. I love the fact that I can speak with passion and hear with conviction in spite of my hearing loss.

So the next time Shane asks, "What kind is it?" I'll tell him, "My brand new digital hearing aids!"

"Set out each day believing in your dreams. Know without a doubt that you were meant for amazing things."

— Josh Hinds

Chapter 34

Building walls inside ourselves isolates hearts from sharing joy or comfort. Interacting with others may be painful sometimes, but withdrawal from humanity creates much worse pain. You're too valuable to be hidden away.

If we share our ration of stones for building bridges instead of walls, then those who come along after us have the chance to use the bridge as a model to boost their self-worth and overcome troubles.

I adapted the poem, "The Touch of the Master's Hand," by Myra Brooks Welch for the hearing impaired. I want to dedicate this poem to the people who have touched my life with the gift of better hearing, speech, and comprehension. I enjoy all these wonderful gifts because someone came in and touched my life with the gift of love.

'Twas battered and scarred, and the auctioneer thought
it barely worth his while,
To waste his time on the old violin,
but he held it up with smile.
"What am I bid for the old violin?
What am I bid?" he cried,
"Who starts the bidding for me?"
"One dollar, do I hear two?

Two dollars, who makes it three?
Three dollars once, three dollars twice,
going for three," but no.
From the back of the room a gray haired man
came forward and picked up the bow.
Then wiping the dust from that old violin
and tightening the frayed, loose strings,
he played a melody, pure and sweet,
even as caroling angels sing.

The music ceased and the auctioneer
with a voice that was quiet and low
said, "What now am I bid for this old violin?"
as he held it aloft with its bow.
"One thousand, one thousand, do I hear two?
Two thousand, who'll make it three?
"Three thousand once, three thousand twice,
going and gone," said he.
The audience cheered but some of them cried,
"We don't understand.
What changed it's worth?" Swift came the reply,
"The touch of the Master's hand."

And many a man with his hearing out of tune
and battered and scarred with a life void of sound,
is auctioned cheap to the thoughtless crowd,
much like this old violin.
Moving lips in a soundless world,
a backward glance, and he travels on.
He's going once, he's going twice,
he's going and almost gone,
But the Master comes and the thoughtless crowd,
they never quite understand
what it's like not to hear, and the change that is wrought
by the touch of the Master's hand.

Many times in my life I have felt like this violin. Maybe you have, too. On a bad day I felt like a dollar. On a better day I felt like two dollars. On a good day I felt like three dollars.

But then someone came in and touched my life, helping me understand that I could reach my greatest dreams and aspirations. Ever since then I've felt like I was worth at least a thousand dollars. On a great day, I feel like two thousand. On a greater day, I feel like three thousand. On a day like today, I feel like a million! I can accomplish whatever I set my heart on. I earned my Master's degree in Business Administration (MBA), I play the violin and viola, I'm a public speaker, I run marathons, I'm an Eagle Scout, and I have a fulfilling career. I've been able to do all these things because someone took the time to reach out and touch my life for the better. A single individual cannot influence every human being on the planet by themselves, but if everyone would simply reach out to just one person, we would create a chain reaction of loving deeds that could race around the planet and change the world.

There are only two kinds of people in this world—those you love and those you don't know yet. The language of love is universal.

My ultimate hero is my Savior, Jesus Christ. He is the one who helped me discover the capabilities that ultimately developed my gifts and talents. I acknowledge God in everything I do, including my failures and success. I give my Heavenly Father all the praise, glory, recognition, and honor.

He has no hands but ours. My mother, father, family, friends, teachers, doctors, hearing specialists, and all those who have touched my life for the better—their hands were all extensions of God's hands. Now I have my hand out to you. More than anything, I want you to believe in your own personal worth. You are of great importance as a human being. No matter what you do for a living, no matter what has happened in your past, no matter what you look like, you are valued.

You are of great worth and are absolutely irreplaceable. I want you to know and believe, with absolutely no doubt, that we are all worthy of love, no matter what size we are. God is no respecter of persons. We should all have respect for one another, no matter what.

Nelson Mandela put it very well when he said, "Our deepest fear is not that we are inadequate. Our deepest fear is that we are

It doesn't matter whether you're an 8' 4" Guatemalan ...

powerful beyond measure. It is our light, not our darkness, that most frightens us. We ask ourselves, who am I to be brilliant, gorgeous, talented, and fabulous? Actually, who are you not to be? You are a child of God. Your playing small doesn't serve the world. There's nothing enlightened about shrinking so that other people won't feel insecure around you.

"We are all meant to shine, as children do. We are born to make manifest the glory of God that is within us. It's not just in some of us, it's in everyone. And as we let our own light shine, we unconsciously give other people permission to do the same. As we are liberated from our own fears, our presence automatically liberates others."

Now I want you to listen to your heart and take out the dream that you have carefully hidden inside. Whatever it is, if it makes you joyful, then go for it! Protect your enthusiasm from the negativity of others. Learn whatever skills you need, and build on whatever talents you have in order to get it. If you go forward with self-confidence and faith in God, you will succeed. Once you're doing what you were meant to do, you will surely enrich the lives of others. You won't be able to help it. Your joy will spill over, and others will want to learn from you.

And so it goes.

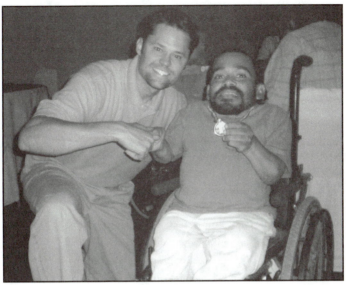

... or a 4′8″ Mexican

I want you to know, as I know, that you are of infinite worth.
You see, you are loved.
Unconditionally.
You can never be unloved. It's not possible, because you have already been touched by the Master's hand.

NOTES

1. Agrilife Extension Texas A&M System, http://fcs.tamu.edu/families/parenting/fathering

2. Federal Interagency Forum on Child and Family Statistics, 1997.

3. Agrilife Extension Texas A&M System, http://fcs.tamu.edu/families/parenting/fathering

4. Amato and Rivera 1999; Bronstein et. al; Marsiglio et. al.

5. http://www.trelease-on-reading.com/rah-ch1.html

6. http://nces.ed.gov/pubsearch/pubsinfo.asp?pubid=2005464

7. http://www.edutopia.org/why-johnny-still-cant-read

8. The Chronicle Review, November 8, 2009

9. http://www.trelease-on-reading.com/rah-ch1.html

10. USA Today, August 8, 2010

11. Early Hearing Detection & Intervention (EHDI) Program http://www.cdc.gov/ncbddd/ehdi/FAQ/questionsgeneralHL.htm)

12. http://www.nidcd.nih.gov/health/inside/spr05/pg1.html

APPENDIX

Justin Osmond
www.justinosmond.com

The Olive Osmond Perpetual Hearing Fund
www.oliveosmond.com

Starkey Hearing Foundation
www.starkeyhearingfoundation.org

Sound Matters
www.soundmatters.com

The Listen Foundation
www.listenfoundation.org

ABOUT THE AUTHORS

Justin Osmond, the second son of Merrill and Mary Osmond, was born with a severe/profound sensorial-neural hearing loss. After being diagnosed at the age of two, he finally got to hear life's precious sounds for his very first time. Considering the fact that he was a couple years behind his peers, he has shown, through intense dedication and mental/physical exertion, that nothing can stop him from going after his dreams and aspirations.

After twelve years of intensive speech/listening therapy, Justin can speak with passion and hear with conviction. There were many obstacles and challenges that represented stumbling blocks, despair, and lack of hope. But his determination, desire, and hope surpassed all hurdles that stood in his way.

Despite the inevitable, and with a 90% hearing loss, Justin pressed forward with a perfect brightness of hope and a love for all humanity. He went on to play the violin, viola, piano, and drums. He has received numerous awards, such as the prestigious Sterling Scholarship in music, academic scholarships, honorary achievements, and many athletic titles in soccer, football, basketball, and track. He is also proud to represent the Boy Scouts of America as an Eagle Scout, and he has earned his Master's in Business Administration (MBA).

Justin currently serves in public relations, as a board member, and the spokesperson for the Starkey Hearing Foundation, the largest outreach program in providing hearing help to children worldwide. He continues to travel the world with one object in mind: *to leave better-hearing smiles behind.*

Justin knows first-hand what it is like to live in a world without sound. He shares his story with the world in order to help all people understand the struggles of being hearing impaired, and know how to overcome them. He lives by his personal motto: *I may have a hearing loss, but that hearing loss does not have me.*

Despite living in the fast lane, his favorite "free time" hobbies include riding his four-wheeler in the mountains, playing with his nieces and nephews, and going for long runs in the foothills. His wholesome country boy smile originates from his love for God, family, and every beautiful thing that bears the fingerprint of the master creator.

Shirley Bahlmann is a prolific author writing in multiple genres, including true pioneer stories, adventure novels, ghostly encounters, how-to, and how-not-to books. This is her sixth biography. *www.shirleybahlmann.com.*